W9-CBT-363

Secrets of a
Private Eye

Secrets of a Private Eye

or, How to Be Your Own Private Investigator

IRWIN BLYE
and ARDY FRIEDBERG

Henry Holt and Company   New York

Copyright © 1987 by Irwin Blye and Ardy Friedberg

All rights reserved, including the right to reproduce this
book or portions thereof in any form.
Published by Henry Holt and Company, Inc.,
521 Fifth Avenue, New York, New York 10175.
Distributed in Canada by Fitzhenry & Whiteside Limited,
195 Allstate Parkway, Markham, Ontario L3R 4T8.

Library of Congress Cataloging-in-Publication Data

Blye, Irwin.
Secrets of a private eye, or, How to be your own
private investigator.
Includes index.
1. Detectives—United States—Handbooks, manuals, etc.
2. Investigations—Handbooks, manuals, etc.
I. Friedberg, Ardy.   II. Title.   III. Title: How to be
your own private investigator.
HV8093.B58   1987   363.2'89   86-14942
ISBN: 0-8050-0370-3

First Edition

Designer: Mary Cregan
Printed in the United States of America
10   9   8   7   6   5   4   3   2   1

ISBN 0-8050-0370-3

For my children, Elizabeth and Anthony

Acknowledgments

I want to thank Victor Juliano, Joseph Durso, Chris Akel, June Mills, Hilary Bezner, and Roberta Cabot for their help in the writing of this book. I also want to thank our editor, Channa Taub, for her encouragement and enthusiasm.

Contents

Secrets of a Private Eye

1

Blye, Private Eye

My name is Irwin Blye. I'm a private investigator. Back in 1976 I wrote a book with Nicholas Pileggi, called *Blye, Private Eye*, in which I used three cases to illustrate the way a private investigator works. I included details on the type of research that goes into a case, an explanation of how those details are tediously assembled into a series of factual conclusions, the legwork involved, the patience necessary on a surveillance, and the pride that comes from the successful conclusion of a case. I tried to give the reader the true flavor of the profession, which is about as far removed from the life of a television or movie private eye as New York is from Kansas City, if you get my meaning.

The publisher of that book sent me out on a promotion tour and I got a tremendous amount of publicity on television (including Johnny Carson and "60 Minutes," no less), on radio talk shows, and in newspapers and magazines. Whenever I was on the air live, whether it was in Duluth or El Paso, the lights on the phones lit up with calls from people who had problems they thought a private investigator could help them solve. The book sold well, and I think it may have served a real purpose by establishing a slightly different image of the real-life private investigator, at least in the minds of those who read it and those who heard me on the air.

That book was published more than ten years ago, but as proof of the public interest in, and the importance of, the subjects I deal with every day, I still get calls from people who have read or heard of the book, I'm invited to appear on at least one television or radio talk show a month, and I'm regularly asked to speak to journalism societies, police associations, community organizations, lawyers' meetings, university classes, and school groups of all ages.

Clearly, a lot of people want to know just what it is a private investigator does and how he or she does it. One thing I have learned over the years is that at one time or another, nearly everyone has the need for the services of a professional private investigator. No one plans on getting a divorce or getting into a settlement dispute or custody battle, but it happens every day. People have accidents, their kids run away, they go into business with people, they inherit estates, they lose property, and on and on. That doesn't mean that everyone goes out and hires a PI (business isn't that good), but a PI's help would make many specific situations a lot easier to handle. These, of course, are only a few of the problems people bring to me each year. There are many more, including criminal matters, of course, but we'll get into all of that in more detail later.

Ten years ago my company, Irwin Blye Investigations, Inc., was just Irwin Blye in a little office with a secretary and two part-time investigators. Today, I've got a secretary and two more, a suite of five offices, three full-time associates, and a dozen or so part-time investigators on call whenever I need them—which happens to be quite often.

Still, things haven't changed all that much. Sure, I'm a whole lot busier, but I still have time to shoot the breeze with my old buddies, take in a ball game, and even enough time to read an occasional mystery novel before bed. I love mysteries, not so much for the tales themselves as for the mistakes the police and the private eyes make in those plots. When you know how to do something really well, it's fun to pick the other person's work apart. Could I do better? Yeah, I'm sure of it and one of these days I've got to get to work and prove it.

Another thing that hasn't changed is the meeting of the board. At least two mornings a week I meet with a very select group of my colleagues for an early breakfast at the very prestigious Grecian

Urn Coffee Shop on Queens Boulevard in the Borough of Queens, New York, one of the counties that make up New York City. We exchange information and gossip, discuss our techniques, tell a few bad jokes, talk about the state of New York's sports teams, and toss around a lot of bull. About a year ago, we were leaving the Urn one morning when my friend Harvey started talking to me about doing another book.

"Irwin, old buddy," he said, "why don't you write the *real* book about being a private investigator? The first one was good, but this time tell the people more about the different types of cases you handle. You can even tell them the inside story of what the business of being a private eye is all about. In fact, tell them that they can do it themselves."

I was intrigued, but I answered, "I don't know, Harvey. The first time it was a lot of work and I don't know if I'm up to doing it again."

But Harvey, like a bloodhound on the scent, was not easily sidetracked. "Take advantage," he urged me. "Use the 'how-to' craze. Make it useful for people, give them some secrets of the trade, show them how to open doors, so to speak.

"I think people would get a bang out of knowing how you really do your job. Look at TV. Look at the movies. Look at the detective magazines. You'll make yourself a small fortune and, of course, I'll take 10 percent off the top for giving you this very superb idea."

"You can forget the 10 percent," I said. "Besides, that kind of thing could put me out of business. If I tell everybody how to investigate their future son-in-law they won't hire me to do it for them. If I tell them how to find the hidden assets of their wives, husbands, and lovers, they won't need me. If I give them the techniques for following someone, everyone will be following someone. I don't want to give the store away."

But Harvey stuck to his guns. I really think he thought he'd get 10 percent. Every time I ate breakfast at the Urn, he would stop me and put the needle in. Finally, he tossed in the kicker. "Look Irwin, the real reason I want you to write a book is that I like to tell my friends to watch my good buddy Irwin, the famous author and private eye, on '60 Minutes.'" He said that with a certain pride that was very good for my ego.

Unlike some of the suggestions I get from my friends (most of them on the fine edge of bad taste), the more Harvey talked, the more what he said sounded like a good idea. Why not do a how-to book? Why not help people do their own investigations? After all, there are how-to's on everything from psychoanalysis to hair cutting. And besides, who am I kidding? I'm not really going to hurt my business. There will still be plenty for me and everybody else. Why not another book? On the other hand, Harvey sold IBM at five dollars and voted for Tom Dewey for president in 1948.

I was now motivated. So, like I'm trained, I started to do a little research, a little private investigating. I made three trips to the library, had conversations with some people in the book business, including an agent and a publicist, and made half a dozen calls to some other PIs around the country. I found out that, sure enough, there isn't a single book out there that is written by a professional investigator for people who want to do their own investigating, their own sleuthing, if you will, in a truly professional way. There are no how-to manuals or workbooks on matrimonial and background investigations. There is nothing between hard or soft covers that says a word about how to look for your runaway son or daughter or how to find your long lost brother. You'll find no help in determining if Uncle Ned is a compulsive gambler who is secretly spending the family fortune, or if the love of your daughter's life is really an escaped mass murderer. I could find nothing that offered advice on how to use the wealth of reference books and information services available for research absolutely free.

And let me tell you some more about what isn't available. There is zero on how to talk to people in a way that gets you the information you want, zip on how to cultivate contacts, or how to use the IRS, the SEC, and other government agencies to do your research for you.

This book, then, was written because there is nothing out there that will fill the woeful information gap, that empty expanse that lies just beyond Ngaio Marsh. This is a different approach to the business of investigating, a guide written by a private investigator that will show the average person how to make use of the techniques of the professionals.

Yes, you the reader, will be able to *do it yourself*. Don't get the wrong idea, however. Let me make it clear from the outset that I don't expect you to be able to do all the things that I do. After all, private investigating is my business. What I'm going to do is share with you some of my experiences and show you the steps I normally take in real cases. Then I'll extract the proven techniques for you to use for yourself. I know that there are many things you can do on your own behalf without jeopardizing your reputation, your bank account, or your health, and those are the things that I'll stress. The idea is to give you a set of tools that will save you time and money.

You may be saying to yourself that this is impossible or illegal or both, but let me set your mind at ease. Far from being impossible, underhanded, or even questionable, all the investigative methods I'm going to reveal, everything I'm going to tell you, in fact, is absolutely legal and completely above board.

So who is this Irwin Blye, and what are his qualifications? Well, let me tell you a bit more about myself. I'm a member of a rare and vanishing breed, a native New Yorker. I was born in the Bronx (and I sound like it), and I went to P.S. 64 on Walton Avenue not far from Yankee Stadium, which probably accounts for my infatuation with baseball and my lifelong love for the Yankees.

That neighborhood certainly had its leavening effects on me, but I didn't really grow up there. I did my real growing up in and around Times Square. My father had a clothing store on Broadway and Fifty-first Street, next to the Capitol Theatre and across the street from Lindy's Restaurant. In those days I used to love to hang out with the salesmen and the tailors in my father's shop. West Fifty-first is not exactly the heart of the theatre district, but it's close by the legendary "Great White Way," and only a few blocks from the seediness of Times Square. My father catered to all types, but most of his clientele were from show business, and I got to meet all of them. I remember one day Mel Torme, the singer, came in for a shirt and my father called him Vic Damone. Torme bought a tie instead of a shirt and after he left the store, I said, "Pop, you insulted the man. That's Mel Torme."

My dad said, "That's OK, he'll like the tie anyway." There are a thousand other stories I could tell, but I won't bore you with them. Suffice it to say that I was exposed to show business and I liked it. Make that I loved it.

Because I hung out so much in my father's store, I ended up

spending a lot of time in Lindy's. I used to eat the strawberry cheesecake (it came with strawberries on top and a bowl of strawberries on the side) and listen to the conversations of George Raft, Joe DiMaggio, and some of the other show business and sports stars who conducted their personal business at those hallowed tables while they too ate cheesecake and Lindy's famous creamed spinach.

For me it was a good life. Occasionally I'd get help on my homework from Zero Mostel, who was good at math, and from time to time Cyclone Anaya, the world heavyweight wrestling champion in those days, would show me one of his favorite moves. I even picked up some spare change running errands and acting as a "gofer." You know, "Irwin, gofer my shirts at the laundry," and "Irwin, gofer some cigars."

I truly loved the atmosphere at Lindy's, but I actually spent more time in Hanson's Drug Store on Seventh Avenue and Fifty-first Street, where almost all of today's famous comedians used to gather for sodas and grilled cheese sandwiches. This was before they got to the big time. Hanson's was a combination soda fountain and coffee shop, and Mr. Hanson catered slavishly to comedians. In those days the regulars at Hanson's counter included Milton Berle, Alan King, Mel Brooks, Buddy Hackett, Lenny Bruce, and half a dozen others, all of whom went on to become famous. I was younger than they were but they let me sit with them while they made each other laugh, and that accounts, at least in part, for my zany sense of humor.

The crowd at Lindy's and Hanson's had a tremendous impact on my young psyche but so did the actors and prizefighters that came into my father's store for the latest in modish outfits. I was so impressed by guys like Kirk Douglas, Kid Gavilan, the Young brothers, and Beau Jack, and the way they talked and strutted around, that I decided at my tender age that I wanted to be an actor. My dad was all for it.

My father asked around and learned that one of the best acting coaches was Betty Cashman, a beautiful and talented woman who was known as the "Coach to the Stars" in those days. She ran an acting school in Carnegie Hall and everybody passed through her school at one time or another. That was in late 1949 and I was fourteen. Betty accepted me, and I became the youngest student in her adult class, which was a real break for me because I was exposed to some budding stars. She believed in a method of acting in which the actor created "the illusion" that he or she was the person in the role. This was antithetical to the then popular Stanislavsky method of "becoming the person" that the role demanded. She eschewed the grunts and groans of Brando and the other Stanislavsky students of the day.

So I began my studies with people like Bruce Gordon, who played Frank Nitti on the old Eliot Ness television series, "The Untouchables," Eric Fleming who went on to star with Clint Eastwood in "Rawhide" on TV, and others who became stars on stage, in the movies, and on television.

I studied with Betty for three years while going to high school during the day, and I got pretty good—good enough in fact to land a small part in the television show "The Greatest Story Ever Told." After that I played the delivery boy in *A Streetcar Named Desire* on the stage and my career seemed on its way.

And what did I do in my spare time? I spent it on the streets, of course. Even in those days, Times Square was not the most savory of neighborhoods, so I got a lot of very real and beneficial street education from the waiters, the hotel clerks and bell boys, the over-the-hill prizefighters, and the "working women" who were, and are, so much a part of the day and nighttime population of the area. They all added to my education in one way or another.

With all my running around, I still managed to graduate from high school and I entered Hofstra University on Long Island. There I hung out with a guy whose uncle owned the Stage Delicatessen, which at that time was probably the best-known delicatessen in New York City. We used to go to the Stage all the time and there I started to meet a new group of people, a number of whom were private investigators. I found them, and the work they did, absolutely fascinating. Just as my experiences at Hanson's had planted in me the seed of show biz, my friends at the Stage planted a new seed. The question was, how was I going to be a private eye and an actor at the same time?

That problem resolved itself. My show-biz career was interrupted permanently when a good movie role fell through (in a film that was to star Montgomery Clift) and I realized, at age eighteen, that there was a lot of uncertainty in the world of show business. I decided college was the place for me to stay if I ever wanted to have any security in my life. I had even considered the clothing business until the day I realized that working for my dad and my uncles, who were partners in the store, was like working for the Marx brothers.

Let me tell you one story that illustrates why I couldn't be in the clothing business. My dad always kept the store open until 10:00 on week nights, and one night at about 9:45 a man came in for a hat. He was a little man, and my father didn't have a small enough size in stock. So instead of saying "Sorry, sir, we don't have anything to fit you right now," he brought out a hat that was at least two sizes too large. To make it appear to fit, my dad put his hand inside the back of the hat as he put it on the man's head. He then carefully steered the gentleman away from the mirror and convinced him that the hat was a perfect fit. The man walked out happy. I couldn't believe my father had done that just to make a sale—though it was very clever. I vowed right there that I would never go into the clothing business.

So when I left college I pursued what had become my second love, the idea of becoming a private investigator. I went to work for a large insurance company as a claims investigator, and it was there that I got my basic training as a private eye. I still have fond memories of that experience, especially my first two assignments.

Our company had received a medical claim from a woman who had burned herself on a radiator, and I was sent out to interview her to find out how and why the accident had happened and to make sure it had, in fact, happened. I called and made an appointment with the woman, who sounded young and very pleasant on the phone. At the appointed time I was on the job. As I knocked on the door of her apartment I felt a surge of excitement. This was my first real investigation. I was wearing a new suit, my shoes were shined, and I was carrying my new briefcase, which contained all my forms, my lunch, and the camera we had all been issued as part of our standard equipment.

When the woman answered the door I was stunned. All the stories I had heard about private eyes flashed through my mind.

She was about twenty-three years old, tall, blond, and absolutely beautiful. In a word, she was a knockout. After a little questioning I learned that she was a dancer at the Copacabana nightclub and that she had sustained her injury when she had accidentally backed into the radiator in her apartment while getting dressed. In other words, her burn, which was causing her physical pain and mental suffering, was on her backside. She showed me the extent of her problem and I examined it closely, and though I was certainly not a specialist in that type of injury, it looked very painful to me.

I had been told during my training that we were to document all injuries with photos so I asked her as delicately as possible if she minded if I took the necessary pictures. As it turned out she was more than happy to let me photograph her burn and, wiping the sweat from my brow, I took pictures from every angle, enough to fill an album. I also took a picture of the offending radiator.

When I got back to the office, I was extremely pleased with myself and couldn't wait for the pictures to be developed. When the messenger brought them from the photo lab I rushed into my boss's office and dropped them on his desk with a flourish. He took one look and yelled, "Blye, you complete jerk, what do you think this is, a porno parlor or an insurance company?"

I was taken aback because I thought I'd done the right thing. All I could say was, "An insurance company, Mr. Gibbons."

Well, old Gibbons read me the proverbial riot act, did everything but wash my mouth out with soap, and told me if I ever did anything that stupid again I was through. Of course, I later learned that the pictures had made the rounds of the office and that in reality I was the envy of the entire staff, many of whom had volunteered to do as much follow-up work on the investigation as necessary, even if it meant working overtime.

The second incident wasn't as pleasant, but it was unusual as well as enlightening—after the fact. The boss sent me out to get a statement from a witness involved in an auto accident case. The man's apartment was on the Lower East Side of Manhattan, the area that for 200 years has been the first place of residence for America's new citizens. It's an old, run-down neighborhood that passed its prime 190 years ago.

The man's apartment was on the sixth floor of one of those walk-up buildings with stairways about three inches wider than your hips. I got there on a late winter afternoon and the outside light was already fading. I pushed open the front door of the building and walked into a tiny lobby strewn with trash. A bare bulb hung from the ceiling. Those sixty watts illuminated enough of the scene for me to see that, besides the trash on the floor, there were two people, covered with newspapers, sound asleep on the stairway. Even with my limited training, I was astute enough to realize that this was going to be a new experience. I made my way up the five flights and after catching my breath, I knocked on the door of apartment 6A. Though the "A" was hanging upside down I felt reasonably certain that it was the right door. There was no answer. I knocked again. This time a male voice growled, "Who is it?"

"My name's Blye," I said brightly. "I'm from the insurance company."

"What do you want from me?" the voice answered.

"I'm here to get a statement on the accident you were in last month on Mulberry Street," I answered.

"Hold it," he said gruffly, and I held it.

The door opened as far as the chain would let it, and I could see part of a very fat, grizzled face with red-rimmed eyes and a three-day stubble. Then he slipped off the chain and opened the door another foot. He was a huge man, not just fat, and powerful-looking. He didn't invite me in.

Thinking it might help matters, I took out my billfold, flipped it open, and showed him my insurance company ID card. He took a quick look at it and said without hesitation, "I ain't talkin' to no insurance cop." With that he spit on the floor and slammed the door on my nose. It hurt like hell. I felt my nose gingerly to see if it was broken. But I didn't bother to knock again.

An hour or so later, after a little time for reflection, the true import of the incident settled on me. My ID card and twenty cents (the going rate in those days) would buy me a cup of coffee. Since that day, I have not shown my ID card to anyone unless it was absolutely necessary.

I stayed out of trouble and continued to progress in the business after that, and two years later I went to work for the New York representative for Lloyd's of London. That was followed by a short stint as an assistant to another private investigator.

I honed my skills on those three jobs and as soon as I was old enough, age twenty-five in New York, I took the state's examination, got my PI license, and opened my own agency.

I have now been a New York State licensed private investigator for over twenty-five years and my clients currently include large and small businesses, lawyers, celebrities, political candidates and parties, government agencies, and private citizens. I recently calculated that I have worked on more than 15,000 cases of nearly every type and description in those twenty-five years and I'm still at it.

2

What Is a Private Eye?

Back in the 1850s and sixties, Americans were still blazing the frontier, and a man named Pinkerton opened the first nationwide private detective service. Since then, his men—variously called the Pinkertons, the Pinkies, and more derogatory names—have been escorting payrolls, patrolling railroad yards, and serving as private guards and private investigators for some of this country's biggest corporations. In the beginning, Mr. Pinkerton used a large, wide open eye in the billboard advertisements he developed to promote his private investigators. The sign said, "The eye that never sleeps." It is now detective lore, though it may be an apocryphal story, that the term "Private Eye" (and afterward "PI") was derived from those ads with the huge eye.

Unblinking eye or not, the people in my profession have been called a lot of less complimentary things through the years, so I'm happy to settle for "private eye," the name Pinkerton seems to have inadvertently created for us.

But beyond the name, I think you should know just what a private eye is and what a private eye does. Without trying to sound too much like the Boy Scout oath, let me tell you that a private eye is diligent, attentive, prepared, resourceful, creative, inquisitive, patient, and neutral. We're even kind enough to help little old ladies across the street occasionally, and unlike our images on television we often speak in complete sentences rather than sustained grunts.

Let me also add that most PIs like to be called private investigators rather than private eyes. The public, however, weaned on Erle Stanley Gardner, *The Maltese Falcon*, and ''Magnum,'' is always going to call us ''private eyes'' no matter what we say. This is especially true of those people afflicted with a touch of the romantic, and what the hell, we all have a little bit of the romantic in us. That's why I too like to think of myself as a ''private eye'' occasionally, especially when I'm on an interesting case that involves the beautiful and the wealthy or the would-be beautiful and wealthy.

In fact, over the years I've had a number of cases that required me to play the fictional version of the PI, but in truth that kind of case, though common in the public mind, is very much out of the ordinary for me. I'm not Philip Marlowe, and my business doesn't usually revolve around clandestine meetings in dimly lit cocktail lounges with beautiful blondes wearing low-cut dresses. I can tell you, however, that it does happen. There are cases that definitely call for that approach, and I can do it (even down to the shoulder holster), though I'm a bit uncomfortable in the part.

For example, I once did a matrimonial investigation for a woman who would not pay me by mail, and it wasn't because she didn't trust the postman. Instead, she insisted on meeting me for lunch in an expensive midtown Manhattan restaurant (she always picked up the tab) where her friends had a chance to see us together. She insisted that I wear a trench coat in the bargain. Then, at some time during our meal, she would give me a conspiratorial look and slip me an envelope containing a check under the table. I would then casually put the envelope in my coat pocket. We played that little game for several months, and I didn't really mind except that I was getting dangerously used to expensive French food.

Another woman came to my office for an initial meeting and as we chatted (I was in shirtsleeves) she noticed that I wasn't wearing a gun and she remarked on it. This is not the least bit out of the ordinary for me because I rarely do carry one. She went on to tell me about her problem—she suspected that one of her employees was taking cash from her dress shop—and then told me she wanted to hire me. Then, with a little blush, she added, "You may think what I'm going to say is a little strange. I want to give you this case. The only problem is, you aren't wearing a gun and private eyes always wear guns. Will you wear one if you work for me?"

I responded shamelessly. "Of course," I said, "I usually wear one anyway," and I wore my gun to all our future meetings.

You don't have to be Sigmund Freud to figure out that both these women were living out little fantasies and that the details, as they imagined them, were extremely important in their minds. I suppose they also had fantasies of car chases, fistfights, gun battles, and hot love scenes—all because of what the fiction writers have done to our image.

There is one colleague of mine, however, who plays the PI role to the absolute hilt. He not only wears a trench coat and a hat with the brim pulled over his eyes, but he talks like Bogart, always has a cigarette dangling from his mouth, carries a "Dirty Harry"–sized cannon, and drives a flashy sports car. That's the way he is with his compatriots so I shudder to think what he must be like when he's with a client.

With this exception, however, I don't know of a single PI who operates anything like those fictionalized versions we all know so well. I'm afraid the romantics will find it disconcerting that most PI's spend their time just like me, doing the drudge work that, in reality, makes up the major part of the professional's day.

But back to my description of the qualities that are required of a real private investigator.

A PI is diligent. In the simplest terms, a private eye is a diligent, sophisticated researcher, not unlike an anthropologist searching for information about ancient civilizations. We both turn over a tremendous number of rocks, peer into dark places, and follow rewarding leads. And there isn't much glamour for either of us until something dramatic is discovered. But in both professions, the basic hard work is an absolute necessity.

Much of an investigator's time is spent weaving his way through the antediluvian systems of giant bureaucracies that unfortunately are more often characterized by indifference, apathy, sloppy paperwork, and outright corruption than by virtue, duty, public service, efficiency, and honesty. When it comes to the major American institutions (banks, insurance companies, public utilities, government agencies, conglomerates, the courts), I'm a middleman who is capable of digging out the data that we all expect to be private.

The fact is, and this will come as a shock to most people, virtually all that information about us that we like to think of as "private" is readily available to anyone who knows where to look. You don't even need to wave around a wad of bills to get intimate details about people's lives because bribery isn't necessary when there are legal procedures for obtaining information built right into the system. Virtually all those "confidential" forms we fill out, all that "personal" data that is keypunched into those "impersonal" whirring computers, are available to anyone who really wants it. We have all been assured that our driver's licenses, our loan forms, our voter registration cards, our employment applications, our credit card information are as secure as Fort Knox. Don't believe it for a second. Give me a shred of information about a person and I can turn it into a biography.

A PI is observant. It is the attention paid to little details that can spell the difference between a successful investigation and one that is merely adequate. Asking the right question at the right time often elicits those details. Our friend from TV, Mr. Columbo, is fond of asking these seemingly minor questions and clarifying obscure points while he scratches his head and shuffles his feet. It works for him and for anyone who is observant, though you must work within the limits of your own personality.

Let me give you an example. A man came to me with the strong suspicion that his wife was having an affair. (You will notice that many of my examples will involve matrimonial matters because nearly 20 percent of my cases are in that area.) We spent a good deal of time going over his wife's regular schedule with him to try to determine when and where she might be having the alleged affair. With that schedule in hand, we began a surveillance. We followed her to her part-time job, to the bank, to the hairdresser, and we still didn't have a clue. She was either very clever or she wasn't having an affair at all. Then one Friday morning we were waiting for her to finish her regular appointment at the beauty shop when I noticed that a number of women who had gone in after her were coming out, and she was still inside. That started me thinking, but nothing really jelled immediately. We followed her again the next Friday and the same thing happened. It seemed strange that she should take twice as long as everyone else, unless . . .

The following week I sent a female operative into the shop after our client's wife had gone in. As our operative was waiting her turn, she noticed that our subject went upstairs with the man who owned the shop. Our operative then got her hair cut, and as she was finishing up nearly forty-five minutes later, our subject came down stairs by herself and left the shop. That, in itself, was not conclusive proof of an affair, but we were able to build a substantial case around those visits and some other facts we uncovered, and our client filed suit and eventually won his matrimonial battle.

What was the story? She had been meeting the hairdresser in his shop every Friday to have her hair done and for their little tryst. No one would ever have known if we hadn't been attentive enough to note that the women who went in the shop after she did came out before she did. That's what I mean by being attentive to the seemingly insignificant details.

A PI is prepared. And, I should add, mentally quick on his feet. This is especially true on surveillance assignments. I always travel with everything I think I could possibly need because I know there will not be time to call "Information" for a much needed phone number, or to check with the office to see if I have the right address, or to go to the bathroom, or to run across the street to get something to eat or drink.

I carry what amounts to a small supply kit with me at all times. I always have a note card with all the vital statistics and phone numbers I think I may need, and if I have a picture of the subject I staple that photo to the back of my index card for handy reference. I'll explain more about this later, but suffice it to say here that it's much better to have something with you that you don't need than to need something you don't have.

I'll also talk more about being quick on your feet, but what I mean in general is cultivating the ability to act and react to a changing situation with ease. You have to maintain your composure and your confidence and be able to switch gears in the heat of the situation. In short, you have to be in command.

A PI is resourceful. I once had a client whose seventeen-year-old daughter was having an affair with a fifty-four-year-old man. Her father wanted the affair stopped for fairly obvious reasons. The father knew very little about the man in question when he hired me to find out the old boy's story. Using the limited information the client gave me, I quickly discovered that the man had a wife, three daughters, and lived comfortably in a lovely house in a suburb north of New York City.

I then had to find out when and where he was meeting my client's young daughter. This meant parking on a quiet suburban street, waiting until the man left home, and then following him by car. In the city this is no problem, but in the suburbs a man sitting alone in a car for any length of time becomes quite obvious. I took the precaution of parking several houses away, but in order to make myself less conspicuous still I filled my car with large cardboard boxes. Then I cut a slit in one of them and sat inside it on the passenger seat. It wasn't very pleasant, but it worked. No one suspected that there was a surveillance going on, and I soon had all the information my client needed to break up his daughter's budding May-December romance. That was perhaps the most resourceful (some might call it weird) action I've ever taken on a case, but I was pleased with myself for thinking of it. Since that time my operatives have used the same ploy any number of times.

A PI is creative. It is often the unexpected that gets results. Serving a subpoena is not something you're likely to be doing, but that is one of the things a PI is often called on to do. A subpoena (a court-ordered appearance for a court case) must be delivered in person and since many people suspect they are going to be served and prefer to avoid the service, one must be creative to get the job done.

You may remember scenes from various movies (mostly those from the thirties and forties that we now call classics) where the court officer knocks on the apartment door and says brightly, "Western Union for Mr. Smith," or "I have a flower delivery for Mrs. Jones."

Unfortunately for process servers, people today are all too aware of these old ploys, so I have created some variations on that theme that are unusual enough to work. The people in my office often use what we call "the old balloon ploy." One of my operatives will show up at the servee's house or apartment with a giant bunch of helium-inflated party balloons. When the unsuspecting servee opens the door he gets not only the balloons, a nice gift in themselves, but also the subpoena. We vary this with a bottle of champagne or a pizza with the works, but the principle is the same. The servee is offered something unusual, which leaves him with his guard down long enough for us to do our job.

We have also acted as waiters in restaurants and presented the subpoena with the check, picked people up in taxis and then served them, dressed as doormen, house painters, and furniture movers, all for the same purpose. We even sent in the clowns on one occasion. It's kind of surprising but, rather than being outraged by our tricks, people often realize they have been beaten, and take it all good-naturedly. Occasionally we do get yelled at or worse (one time I was sprayed with a garden hose), but that's all part of the job.

Speaking of serving subpoenas, a woman once asked me to serve a subpoena on her husband by going out on the ledge of his office building and crawling from the office window next door to his window, which was always open. In fact, she offered me $500 extra to do it. The money was certainly enticing; unfortunately, I had to refuse for two reasons. The first is that I have vertigo (this was a twelfth-floor ledge), and the second is that even if heights didn't bother me, I was scared to crawl out on that ledge anyway.

At that point, this otherwise very nice and well-mannered lady turned into a monster. She screamed at me, called me a coward, made some other comments about my manhood, and then grabbed the subpoena from my hand and said she would do it herself. I told her that the service wouldn't be valid because she was a party to the case, and that it would have to be done all over again, but she didn't give a damn at the time. She certainly caught her husband by surprise when she tapped him on the shoulder from the window ledge, and she made me look like a wimp, but her efforts were in vain as I had warned her they would be.

The point here is, since there are no real rules to the game of investigation, anything goes. An active imagination can spell the difference between success and frustration.

A PI is inquisitive. Curiosity may have killed the cat, but inquisitiveness has saved the day for many a private eye. To be effective and thorough, you usually have to look behind and around the things you see and hear to get information you need.

I was once hired to find witnesses to an auto accident that occurred on the Long Island Expressway, which leads from New York City to the suburbs of Long Island. It is one of the country's busiest highways and carries tens of thousands of cars every day. After several days of fruitless searching that included a complete canvass of all the houses that faced the highway in the immediate area, it seemed we had exhausted all our possibilities.

Still, for some reason I decided to go out to the site once more on the off chance that I would run across something we hadn't seen before or someone we hadn't talked with before. As I stood by the road, I happened to look up and I noticed a house that I hadn't spotted before because it was well back from the road, perhaps as much as half a mile, and partially hidden by trees. I could see, however, that the large windows of that house had an unobstructed view of the highway. I told myself, "What the hell, it can't hurt to try." So I drove over and knocked on the door. An elderly man answered, and I told him my story, including the date and time the accident took place.

He looked at me as if I was some sort of mind reader and quickly ushered me into the house. As we walked into his front room I saw one of those long spyglasses mounted on a tripod. It was pointed out the window and down toward the highway. The old gentleman explained to me that he loved to look at the highway and watch the cars and that, in fact, he had been looking at the road at the precise time of the accident and had seen it all. It was his written statement that served to clear my client, who had been charged with negligence. If I hadn't been inquisitive enough to take that last trip, I don't think we'd have won the case.

If you learn to observe and to ask the same questions that a journalist would ask—who, what, when, where, why, and how—you will eventually uncover just about everything you need. Pretend you're Mike Wallace, hot on the heels of a great story. And while you're at it, learn another journalistic trick. Cultivate the ability to read upside down. This will allow you to read documents, letters, and notes on desks and in people's hands, all of which can be very informative.

A PI is patient. I have to keep reminding myself that most things don't happen quickly in this business, because I'd prefer that they did. A surveillance can take ten hours or ten days; the average is around five days. One telephone call may provide a mass of information, and fifty calls may provide zero. A mail inquiry can take as long as two months and sometimes longer if you're writing a government agency. It once took me nine months to get a reply to a simple request for a training manual from the United States Army.

My longest running case lasted nearly two years. It was a matrimonial situation. The wife—a wealthy woman—had hired me because she suspected her husband was cheating on her and she wanted to prove it as grounds for divorce. She wanted out of the marriage in the worst way. At the outset I followed the husband for thirty straight days and found absolutely no evidence to support her suspicions. Usually, a person having an affair will see his or her lover every two or three days. It's a rare situation where the two people meet only once a week or once every two weeks. It's the nature of the beast. People having an affair want to get together as often as possible. Therefore, it didn't seem to me that the woman was on the right track.

I presented her with a complete report on my long surveillance and told her I thought she'd be wasting her money to continue the investigation. She didn't agree. She put me on a retainer and told me to stay on the case part-time until further notice. I did. Someone from my office tailed this poor guy off and on for another year and eight months. We made periodic reports to the woman, and she paid us regularly.

We never did find her husband in a compromising or even questionable situation. I was firmly convinced, and had been for a long time, that the guy was straight as an arrow, and I finally told her that I wasn't interested in pursuing the case any further. She was incensed because she was still sure he was a philanderer, evidence or no. She nearly booted me out of her house the last time we met, and as I was heading for my car she stood at the front door and shouted obscenities at me for not being able to prove her suspicions. I'd bet that she hired another investigator to continue the case, and she may still be having the poor guy followed after all these years.

In this case the client had more patience than even I did, but I showed my perseverance by beating that dead horse for nearly two years. Remember, though, the point is this: Impatience is a vice and patience is a virtue.

A PI is neutral. During the years I've been in practice I have dealt with cases that encompass the entire economic and social spectrum of American society. I've handled complicated estate cases for the very rich, grimy matrimonial investigations, insurance claims, missing persons, backgrounds and locates, petty theft, and more serious crimes that included armed robbery, rape, and murder. Regardless of the case, however, I've always tried, and I think I've always succeeded, to remain neutral. I simply don't decide on guilt or innocence. On a moral basis, who am I to sit in judgment of anyone? Besides, if I were to get emotionally involved it would spell serious trouble for me and the client. But believe me, it's not always easy to stay aloof or neutral.

I know that for those of you who make use of this book to conduct your own investigations establishing your neutrality and maintaining your detachment are going to be difficult. You are most likely going to have a vested emotional interest in the outcome of what you're doing.

Let's say, for example, you suspect your husband or wife of having an affair. Imagine the following scenario. You follow your spouse to an apartment building, perhaps (as is often the case) the apartment building of a good friend of yours. (Yes, friends are often involved in extramarital affairs.) You station yourself outside and a little while later your spouse and another person walk out of that building arm in arm and head up the street. Do you run after them screaming in rage? Do you stand there with your mouth open? Do you bite your lip and clench your fists? These are all the natural reactions of an involved person, but not the reactions of a PI. If I were keeping that surveillance, I'd have no problem staying cool because I'm not involved personally. If you are going to conduct your own investigation, you need to keep in mind that it is likely to be hard for you to remain neutral.

Still, even I sometimes find it hard to remain neutral. I had a case in which a convicted rapist who had been released from a mental hospital committed another rape. I was hired by the attorney of the accused man to find information that would be beneficial to his case. I had absolutely no sympathy for the rapist, but the lawyer and I had worked together on a number of cases in the past so I took the case.

What I found in my investigation was that the accused was a Vietnam veteran who had seen a lot of jungle combat. He had returned to the States, and like so many other vets, had been unable to find a permanent job. His wife divorced him and then, some months later, he had been arrested and convicted of rape. Because he was a veteran he was sentenced to two years of psychiatric treatment. After that he had been released as cured. When the alleged rape took place he was driving a taxi. The testimony he had given to his lawyer indicated that he admitted to having had sexual relations with the victim in his cab after he had picked her up as a fare. His story was that she had lured him into the act in the backseat of the cab.

I also investigated the woman's background. It turned out that she came from a nice family, that she was a sales representative for a cosmetics company, was unmarried, and that there was nothing strange in her medical history. All of her friends spoke highly of her, and no one indicated that she was a heavy drinker or a drug user. She was clean.

I've investigated hundreds of rape cases, and based on what I knew about the accused and what I had learned about the victim, I didn't buy a word of his story. In fact, I was sure the guy was guilty. But after interviewing the doctors who had treated him and about a dozen other people involved in his life up to that point, I discovered that there was a potentially mitigating circumstance. The man, for a number of fairly sound psychological reasons, was apparently not able to tell right from wrong. It seemed plausible that he thought that she had "led him on." I presented these facts to the lawyer, and suggested that the man be given a polygraph test. He passed two tests—it seemed he really believed she wanted to have sex with him. The man was eventually sent back for additional psychiatric treatment rather than being sent to prison. The woman received substantial financial restitution.

I disliked that job. My sympathies were clearly with the woman. I was convinced that there was no justification for turning this man loose in the first place. But that wasn't the issue. What was at issue was his mental state at the time of the incident, and I had been hired to establish the truth. I had tried to remain professionally neutral, and I had been successful as far as the job itself was concerned. Personally I did not feel the least bit neutral—but that is one of the hazards of the job.

There is also another kind of neutrality. About five years ago I was working on a criminal case that involved a group of alleged mob figures. During my investigation I was asked to meet with a man who was supposed to be important to the case of the defendants. As it turned out, he certainly was important. He was a "bagman" for the mob, though I didn't know it when our meeting was scheduled. A bagman carries money between parties, money that is used to buy favors.

We met in Battery Park in Lower Manhattan one summer afternoon, and as we sat talking on a bench and looking across New York harbor out at the Statue of Liberty, he took an envelope out of his inside pocket. He put it on the bench and pushed it toward me. "There's twenty-five thousand in cash inside," he said casually, "and all you have to do to earn it is forget that you were ever involved in this case."

Perhaps under the influence of the statue in the harbor, I pushed it back toward him without hesitation and said simply, "I can't do that because I'm already involved."

"That's understandable," he said, with a businesslike grasp of my position as another man just doing his job, and he put the envelope back in his pocket. For a few minutes more we talked about the view and the weather, and then he got up and left. I never saw him again.

The moral here is that it's not always easy to be neutral or even honest. I've been in this sort of compromising situation more than once and I haven't succumbed yet and I have no intention of doing so in the future. But as you can see, there can be temptations. Fortunately, it's not the sort of thing that happens every day or even every year. If it were, I'm not sure I could take the stress.

All of the qualities I've just talked about are essential ingredients in the makeup of a successful, professional PI. Some private investigators have them and some don't. Very few people have them all, but it is the man or woman who can put a combination of these talents and skills to work who will be successful in the long run.

3

The Importance of Attitude and Some Rules of the Game

I know that there are going to be a number of things in this book that will cause you to ask yourself: "How on earth can I possibly do that?"

Your concern is certainly valid: Some of the suggestions here require not only a lot of time but a good deal of guts, determination, and creativity to carry through successfully.

Following your spouse, for example, can be a difficult task physically and emotionally because you are very much involved.

Proving that dear old Aunt Nellie was incompetent when she left all her money to the ASPCA can be an unpleasant task. After all, she was a wonderful old woman, if a bit dotty, and you're going to have to do and say some things that will put her in a bad light.

Trying to find your natural parents is not only hard work but psychologically draining as well. You have to be torn by doubts about what you're doing, and you will wonder how you're going to react when you find your mother or father. And what do you do if it doesn't work out well?

Discovering that your teenager is using drugs and that he is getting them from little Frankie down the block is an emotional shock. Where did you go wrong? Who's to blame? Will helping your kid mean throwing Frankie to the wolves?

To do these things you need to be highly motivated; you must want to do them. If you tell yourself, "This is too much trouble," then you lack the necessary motivation and the job probably isn't important anyway. As a professional, I'm paid for what I do and that is usually, though not always, my motivation. As an amateur you won't be getting paid a cent, so you need something more. What makes it possible for you to do your job is the fact that you *are* personally involved and that you *want* and *need* to do it. This is the best type of motivation. If you want and need to know badly enough, you will be able to sweep aside the "How can I do that?" feelings without too much difficulty. At that point you'll be able to tell yourself to go ahead and uncover the facts, whatever they may indicate, and you'll be as creative as need be in doing it.

By God, if Mary, your wife of twenty-two years, is cheating on you, you're going to *want* to find out how, when, where, and with whom. If Aunt Nellie left a million bucks to the ASPCA and $139 to you when you thought you were her favorite nephew, you're going to go after your share of that cash even if you have to make her look like a doddering, slobbering, senile old fool. If you've always wondered about the circumstances surrounding your adoption, you're going to dig until you find your roots and let the chips fall where they may. And if you suspect that it is not an overdose of homework that has your thirteen-year-old nodding out at dinner, you aren't going to stop until you get to the bottom of the problem. These are the motivations of the amateur investigator and they are strong ones, strong enough to carry you through until the job is done.

Once you're motivated, once you've convinced yourself of your need and desire to know, you should be aware of a few additional reminders that I use as working guidelines. Through my experience, I have developed these rules that I use in every case. They will be invaluable to you in virtually every situation. I live by these guidelines, and though you need not make that kind of commitment, I suspect you will adhere to them the way I do when you understand their importance.

NUMBER 1: NEVER ASSUME ANYTHING

This rule is number one in importance. And when I say *never* assume anything, I mean *anything*. Here are two examples that illustrate the point.

The first involves a matrimonial case. A middle-aged woman, separated from her husband for several years, came to my office and asked me to put her husband under surveillance because she was sure that he was seeing a younger woman. She told me she hadn't minded being separated and going her own way, but she resented him paying attention to a "slut," as she referred to the woman. I took the job, and she and I went to her husband's place of business so that I could get a good look at him before taking up the surveillance.

The husband's store was in a shopping mall in the lower concourse of an office building. As we watched from a spot where we wouldn't be noticed, the wife pointed to one of the men inside behind the counter and said without a second's hesitation, "That's him. The one with the blue sweater. That's the cheating son of a bitch." There was only one man with a blue sweater where she was looking, so clearly that was my man. I took a long look and then we left.

That evening I came back and waited for him to close up the store. Then I followed him by car from midtown Manhattan into suburban New Jersey. We had been on the road about forty-five minutes when he pulled up and parked in front of a small apartment building. He went in and since he didn't know me, I followed him right inside. I hung back a few steps and let him get in the elevator. Since he was the only person in the elevator, I knew that when it stopped it would be his floor. The elevator light stopped at four and then the car came back down. I took it up to double-check the identification. But to play it safe, I did what I always do. I rode up to the sixth floor and walked down to four. Sometimes I'll get off a floor below where I'm headed and sometimes I'll walk up the entire distance. This is a good way to avoid being spotted, and you can always pretend you're a tenant walking the stairs for exercise. At any rate, I checked the names on all the apartment doors on the fourth floor, but none of them matched the name I had been given. I went back downstairs and checked the mailboxes, but his name was not there either. People normally don't change their names, so I knew something was wrong.

The first thing the next morning I checked with the motor vehicles department for the owner of the license plate number I'd gotten off the car my subject had driven the night before. The name matched the name on the apartment door, not the name of my subject. I called the wife, my client, and told her what had happened.

"That's impossible," she exploded. "You followed the wrong man. You were with me. I pointed him out to you. You knew what he looked like. Don't you think I know what my own husband looks like when I see him?"

I didn't say what I wanted to say in answer to that question. "True enough," I said, "but I think you identified the wrong man. Could it be? Think about it for a minute."

She was upset, angry, to be precise, and she demanded that we meet at the shopping mall again that afternoon so she could prove her point and make me out for the idiot I surely was. She said vehemently, "After all I should know the man I lived with for nearly thirty years."

"That's absolutely true," I said, trying not to sound too sarcastic. We made arrangements to meet again later that day.

At four-thirty the woman and I met at the entrance to the shopping concourse, and she gave me a stare that would have turned a lesser man to salt. Then we walked to the spot where we had stood the day before. We hadn't been watching the shop for two minutes when she threw her hands up to her mouth and stifled a little yelp of discovery.

"Mr. Blye, I'm so sorry," she said in such an abject way that I sympathized with her. "You're absolutely right. I haven't seen Fred for a while and I identified the wrong person. That's him over there in the corner, the one with the beard. Please forgive me. I'm very stupid."

I nodded in agreement, but I was almost as mad at myself as I was at her. I had assumed the woman would be able to identify her husband. This is an extreme case, but it proves the importance of this guideline beyond a shadow of a doubt. After all, it's more than reasonable to assume that a wife can accurately identify her husband of thirty years. So, the point is made—never assume.

The other case that illustrates this point very convincingly involved a marriage license. A widow came to me because her ex-husband's second wife was claiming part of the deceased's rather sizable estate. She was convinced that the man had never actually remarried even though the other woman had given a marriage license to her attorney as proof.

I called the second wife, and she was as convinced that she had been legally married as the first wife was that the second marriage wasn't valid. The second wedding had supposedly taken place in a little town in Maryland, and I sent an investigator there to check the public records and find some witnesses to prove where and when the event had taken place.

After three days my operative returned and reported that she could not find a church, a minister, a witness, or a registered document in the courthouse that would prove that the second wife's marriage certificate was valid. We went over all the possibilities and determined on the evidence we had that the woman in Maryland had apparently been duped by her "husband." Though we could never prove it, it seemed clear that he must have arranged a phony ceremony, hired a bogus minister, paid fake witnesses, and given her a false marriage license.

I know that counterfeit college degrees and fake ID cards are available all over the country. A person can become a Doctor of Catastrophe (D.C.) or an ordained minister in the Church of the Light-Headed for a price, often a small price. And I also knew that marriage licenses were for sale. Still, I had assumed, and the ex-wife's lawyer had assumed, that the license in the lawyer's possession was legitimate. The first wife had a feeling that the whole thing was out of order, and she was absolutely right. Again, never assume.

NUMBER 2: THERE IS NO SUCH THING AS PRIVACY

I can find out almost anything I want to know about you, your neighbor, your business partner, your son-in-law, or your grandfather. It's a shocking revelation, but the vaunted right to privacy, a keystone in the American system, is a myth. Just think about it for a minute. When you get a driver's license, and nearly every American has one, you have to fill out a form. On that form you give your name, address, date of birth, height, weight, color of eyes, identifying marks, whether you wear glasses or contact lenses for driving, if you've had previous violations, and the penalties for those violations. Undoubtedly, you think this information is confidential.

Well, let me tell you, it isn't. I can get it, you can get it, anyone can get it by filing a simple form with the state motor vehicles department and paying a nominal fee. If this were all the information I could get on a person it would be enough to lead me to much more.

A couple of years ago I was working on a case involving a national newspaper known for its shocking (some might say scandalous) behavior in putting stories together. This particular case involved what the paper had said about a major figure in the entertainment world, and it resulted in a giant libel suit against the paper.

One of the key sources for the story was a waiter in a French restaurant in Chevy Chase, Maryland, where the celebrity was said to have been drunk and disorderly. The waiter was an itinerant worker, and when I got the assignment he had long since left the restaurant for parts unknown. I did have his name and his date of birth because he had been paid by the restaurant and they had that information on record. With this meager bit of data I was able to get the information on his driver's license. The address and description on the license led me along a circuitous route from Washington, D.C., to Raleigh, North Carolina, to Detroit, and finally to Chicago, where I found him working under an assumed name in another French restaurant.

A driver's license is a good "confidential" source, but it is only one source of "confidential" information available on people. Here is an abbreviated list of sources that people think are confidential: the courts, Social Security, law enforcement agencies, public assistance, banks, credit card and insurance companies, loan companies and credit bureaus, employers, tax records, the phone company, the military, and schools at all levels.

Virtually everything that is written down is available to anyone who has a desire for it. A while back I appeared on the MacNeil-Lehrer news program on public television along with the president of a large, well-known, and widely advertised insurance company. During the conversation the subject of confidentiality was raised.

Robert MacNeil asked, "Mr. Blye, could you get confidential information from Mr. Smith's [not his real name] insurance company or any other insurance company if you wanted it?"

"Of course," I said. "I do it all the time and if Mr. Smith would like me to tell him how, I'll be glad to do it off camera after the show."

"Is this true, Mr. Smith?" MacNeil asked.

"Yes, I'm afraid it is," Smith answered, "but we do try to safeguard a policy owner's personal information as much as possible."

It had to be clear to anyone who was paying attention that the so-called personal, private, confidential information held by that company (and virtually all other companies) could become public knowledge with the simple dialing of a telephone. This revelation doesn't shock me because I know that all the giant organizations are run by a lot of little people. There are weak links in that chain of people and you just have to be able to exploit them.

Information from government agencies, insurance companies, loan companies, even banks is accessible legally and without misrepresentation. You just have to know how to do it. The jargon and the turns of phrase that are peculiar to certain fields are the keys to this information kingdom. For example, when I'm doing a financial check I'll generally call the bank or banks involved, introduce myself, and ask if I can have the "standard form XYZ" on so-and-so. If I say that, the information flows. If, on the other hand, I didn't know the form number, I'd get a curt reply if I was lucky enough to get a reply at all.

While you ponder the enormity of the fact that all of this information is available on you, let me add that computerization has made access to this information faster and more complete than ever before. I'll talk more about this later, but for now, consider that intimate details of your life exist on whirring computer tapes and that those tapes often spill their proverbial guts when the right button is pushed.

NUMBER 3: THERE ARE NO SHORTCUTS

Have you ever noticed that the cops who are on stakeouts in the movies and on TV are never tired, hungry, or have to go to the bathroom? That's because they usually only have to wait a minute or two for their pigeon to fly by. Since the viewing audience can't be expected to sit through a seven-hour stakeout, real time has to be compressed into a few minutes in order to keep the viewer from switching channels. We all understand that this sort of innocent deception is necessary for dramatic effect, but don't be suckered into thinking that this is the way things really are. There are no shortcuts in an investigation, not on a stakeout or in any other part of the job.

So you may have to sit in your car for those seven hours, or spend seven hours at the courthouse looking through documents, or walk the streets for seven hours knocking on doors to get information. That's the name of the game.

I say this because I don't want you to get the idea that the information I'm going to give you in this book provides a quick fix. I don't have a panacea or a gold key to some magic domain where data banks gush information and people trample each other to help you. In fact, I can't think of anything we're going to talk about that happens—unless you're extremely lucky—with a snap of the fingers.

How long do things take, you ask? There is no way to estimate, no average time, because these processes vary too much from case to case. But you can bank on one thing—everything will take longer than you think it should.

For example, if you write to the motor vehicles department for license information it may take three to six weeks to get an answer. Getting a forwarding address from the post office can take five minutes or half a day. You can spend the better part of an afternoon trying to get through to some places on the telephone, for God's sake.

What I'm trying to say is this. Don't let yourself fall into the trap of thinking a few minutes here and a few minutes there will get the job done—everything takes time. If it were all so easy, there wouldn't be any need for professional private investigators.

NUMBER 4: THE ONLY SHORTCUT IS KNOWLEDGE

OK, so I fudged a little. Yes, there is one shortcut, but it is only a shortcut after you've worked hard to get to it. In other words, you arrive at this shortcut through heavy traffic. Knowledge is that shortcut.

The kind of knowledge I'm talking about is that first real breakthrough that shows you're on the right track. Say you're looking for a missing document—the deed to your mother's house in Topeka, Kansas, for example. You checked the safety deposit box and found nothing but antique costume jewelry. You then tried to get in touch with the title insurance company only to find out that they went out of business fifteen years ago and turned their files over to a bank. A call to that bank reveals that it has also gone out of business. This represents three serious dead ends, and it may have taken a month or more to reach that point in the road.

Then, in a pile of other documents in the old rolltop desk, you discover the name of the lawyer who handled the closing on the house so many years ago. This little piece of knowledge is what will now, quite easily, lead you to the document you are seeking. Even if that lawyer is dead and his office has been closed for a decade, you will be able to track down his records by contacting the state bar association or finding his former partners, or through the courts in Topeka. I think you can see that this kind of knowledge is a shortcut but that it was reached the long way around.

Part of my skill is in developing a varied cast of friends and acquaintances, a variety of sources and resources that can provide leads and information on virtually any subject. This spectrum of characters includes policemen on the beat, detectives, federal agents, court clerks, probation officers, prosecutors, tipsters, licensed and unlicensed PIs, lawyers, doctors, show biz personalities, sports stars, boxing promoters, doormen and mailmen, and some wealthy people and high-placed officers in large multinational corporations who, for obvious reasons, always remain anonymous.

I realize that my contacts are unique, but anyone can get to know a doorman. You don't have to be too aggressive to meet the milkman or mailman. The clerk in the courthouse, the garbage man, and the neighbors are just people after all, and many of them want to be friendly. Today, most of us have friends who are doctors and lawyers, insurance agents and accountants, and these people can all provide information that you can use to your advantage when necessary. I also use books as sources of information. From the telephone directory to *Who's Who in Japan*, these books are wonderful for quick reference, and carefully mined, they can provide a wealth of information. Information is power, it has been said, and I agree.

I know that the public has this fantasy idea about mysteries, but I have come to realize that in real life there aren't many true mysteries. I deal in situations where some, or many, of the facts are missing and this missing information is what constitutes the "mystery." To me, though, the missing facts don't represent a mystery at all, only something that is missing, something I'm sure will eventually be found.

And unlike the classic, one-hour television show, my type of drama, if you can call it that, isn't solved in a single meeting. Basic and awful truths don't emerge from sudden and cathartic revelations in my office, in front of the police, in the courtroom, or in the judge's chambers. It takes time, patience, and a knowledge of the truth. I can't give you the patience, but I can give you some of the tricks of the trade, hints that you can use and that will serve as the basis for ideas and approaches you will develop on your own.

Information is the key. To get where you're going, you have to be able to get information, and that means dealing with people. And therein lies the real secret. In dealing with people you have to be able to make yourself liked while masking the fact that you want a little information. Of course you may also have to mask the fact that you can't stand the person you're talking with. You have to be polite and have a ready smile. You shouldn't be a physical or psychological threat to anyone. You have to be the audience, not the performer. And it's not just knowing how to talk to people, you have to know how to read them as well.

Eventually this skill develops to the point where people don't have to say a word and you know a certain amount about them. I look at their clothes, the job they do, the way they sit or stand, how they act with those around them, and I listen carefully to the tone of their voices. You have to size people up in order to get information, and you have to do it quickly. Then, your assessment made, you have to plunge in, play your role, respond like a fencer, parry, and then thrust home.

I think that being a private eye is a special job with special requirements. I've learned to thread my way through the intricacies of the bureaucracy like a halfback running to daylight. I can play the computer like a concert pianist. I can manipulate red tape without having any of it stick to my fingers. My skill, even my genius, if you'll pardon the self-praise, lies in this ability to find the missing details, focus on them, and then use the gigantic American bureaucracy.

Where most people are baffled by the impersonal layers of bureaucrats and bureaucratese and the irrational delays inherent in those layers, I've learned to manipulate them and turn the bureaucracy back on itself. I have an undergraduate degree in the basics of paperwork. I have a master's degree in the technical field of using government information forms. I have a doctorate in the infrastructure of bureaucratic organizations. It is this bureaucracy that holds the answers to almost all questions. The secret lies in knowing how to trigger those great impersonal machines to cough up the right information in a reasonable length of time.

There are any number of legitimate ways to get information, and they're available to anyone in this country who has the time and inclination to go after them. The state motor vehicles department, the tax collector, the store clerk, the bank officer, the credit manager, the telephone installer, and the minister are all invaluable sources of information. To put it straight, with an ounce of effort you can find out just about anything you want to know about anybody, anywhere.

Here's a little hint to keep in mind. The two most valuable pieces of knowledge, the two best shortcuts you can have besides a name, are a current or former address and a Social Security number. Information flows like water from these little pieces of data. I find the best means of identification is the Social Security number. In the next few years, I'm told, your Social Security number will be used for identification on almost every document. There is talk, in fact, that all the other identification numbers we carry will be replaced by it.

NUMBER 5: DON'T WEAR BLINDERS

Horses wear blinders to keep them from looking to the side and getting confused and distracted by the other horses and jockeys in a race. This is sometimes good for humans—when absolute attention to a single detail is necessary—but it isn't good in the business of research and investigation.

Unfortunately, all too often we humans do wear blinders. We simply fail to see the big picture. I've found over the years that during an investigation I can develop a severe case of tunnel vision; I wind up seeing only what is straight ahead of me and not some of the interesting and important things that are just off to the side. That's because I'm totally focused, looking for one thing, and I'm not going to be deterred. The only thing wrong with this approach is that all sorts of important things may be happening all around me, and because I have such a narrow focus, such a restricted field of vision, because my blinders prevent me from looking sideways, I don't see those things that could be helpful to my case.

The message is, then, don't look only at what is directly in front of you. It's a mistake in investigative work, and it's a mistake in most things. If you're researching, don't stop looking when you have that one specific piece of information. It may be the answer to your immediate question, but ask yourself about the next step, about what more you could do, where you could look for more information.

The ability to do this effectively is what makes for successful private investigators. We aren't private eyes or private detectives, we're private investigators and the word "investigator" means researcher. Simply put, we're well-paid finders of facts, and if we don't trade on this talent then the work we do is no more skilled than that of the kid writing an essay on his summer vacation.

My colleague Joe has the talent to shed the blinders. During the last couple of years he has been working on a murder case with strange overtones. He was getting nowhere and then he thought of hiring an expert in the way blood spatters, a man who has spent his professional life studying how blood spatters and the specific things that cause it to spatter in different patterns. A gunshot, a knife wound, a fall, a blow with the fist, all cause a person's blood to spatter. The shape, size, and formation of that spatter are indicative of what went on and what happened after the wound was inflicted. To make a long story short, the blood expert's findings broke the case.

Calling in this expert was a brilliant move on Joe's part. Joe wasn't so intent on one aspect of his investigation that he couldn't step back and ask himself about the next step. So do as Joe does. Talk to yourself. Ask yourself questions. There is a way; you just have to find it. If the street is blocked, don't turn and go up a dead end. Instead, turn onto the boulevard and you'll find several side streets that could be rewarding.

One other point on wearing blinders. An attitude about a person or a place can effectively put a very opaque set of blinders over your eyes. If you don't like someone, don't like a neighborhood, don't think you can get along in a certain situation, you become immobilized and negative.

I remember a case that took me to the lowest part of the Lower East Side in Manhattan. This is a neighborhood where you have to be tough just to go to the grocery for a container of milk. I needed to get a statement from a witness in a manslaughter case, so I hopped in a cab and told the driver the address. He said, "You crazy. I ain't goin' ta Avnuh C fer nobody."

This did not reassure me, but I said, "I'll make a deal with you. Take me to Second Avenue and Sixth Street and I'll walk from there." He grudgingly agreed.

That walk is not particularly scenic in the aesthetic sense, but it's filled with all kinds of scenery. And it isn't long in distance, but it is very long in time. There are drug deals being made on nearly every corner. The junkies who aren't buying or selling are nodding out in doorways. People and sirens are screaming constantly. The streets and sidewalks are covered with trash. The Hell's Angels are holding an open-air meeting. All the time, decent people, and private investigators, try to pick their way around and through this flotsam and jetsam in an effort to conduct a normal life and normal business.

At any rate, I found the address. On the front stoop of the building, four hulks dressed in black leather and red headbands were arrayed in battle formation, and two more of their friends were sitting on top of a nearby car picking paint off the roof with hunting knives.

This is where you ask yourself if you have the right attitude to carry through on a case. A karate champion would ask himself the same question. A member of the Special Forces might feel a little insecure. So, naturally, I debated with myself as I walked toward this formidable bunch. I knew my man was inside that building, and I also knew he wasn't going to be a pussycat himself. He might take a swing at me just for being on the block. I could have chucked it but I didn't. I walked past those dudes like they weren't there and clumped up the stairs to the fourth floor like I owned the building. I got the statement I needed.

The message? Take off your blinders and open your eyes. Take that extra step and don't let your attitude get in the way.

NUMBER 6: RELY ON YOUR INSTINCTS

I'm a firm believer in instinct. If I wake up in the morning with a number in my head, I'll play it in the lottery that afternoon. When I go to the races, I pick my horses by instinct. If I like the look in a horse's eyes I'll plunk down two bucks on his nose. I haven't ever won the lottery, and I rarely win at the races, but I know that one of these days my instinct is going to pay off big. But seriously, I think you have to listen to that inner voice whispering sweet nothings. Of course, your instincts won't always be right, but you can trust them, I believe, at least 70 percent of the time.

Last summer I was on a surveillance with a partner. We were parked in front of a large office building. We were hired to keep an eye on an executive who was suspected of embezzling funds from his company. We had a picture of the man, and we were going to use it to identify him. We'd been told that he would be wearing a suit and tie, probably a hat, and would be carrying a briefcase. As we watched, a guy came out of the revolving doors dressed in a windbreaker and carrying a shopping bag. My instincts said that was our man, but his clothes didn't even come close to the description we'd been given.

My partner and I looked at each other. "That's him," I said.

Sal said, "It can't be. Look at the way he's dressed."

"What do we do?" I asked.

"He just doesn't fit the description in any way," Sal said, "so let's sit tight."

"I still think that's him," I repeated, but we didn't follow. It was the wrong decision. We sat for another hour and our man didn't show. Later we learned that the fellow with the shopping bag was our subject. He had slipped by, and we lost half a day on the job. My instincts had been right. Sometimes you have to take chances and follow those instincts.

I'm sure you often get a flash of insight when you're talking to someone. You realize, after sizing them up quickly, that you have to use a certain approach, a certain tone of voice, be firm, be humorous or whatever, and you do it. It may be a risk at times but you have to depend on that instinct; more often than not, you're absolutely on target.

NUMBER 7: BE ACCURATE

Nothing destroys a case like an inaccurate report. All can be lost if you have the wrong date, if the time of day is way off, or if you don't note the particulars of a situation as precisely as possible. On the other hand, remember that you're not writing a novel or getting paid by the word for the length of your notes.

I once fired an investigator because he carried his descriptions and accounts of incidents and locations well past both the sublime and the ridiculous. The last straw was his surveillance report that read:

> Followed subject to apartment building on NW corner of Fifth Avenue and 56th Street. It was a 42-story, red brick structure with a glass-enclosed, two-story lobby. The doorman was a male Caucasian, about 40 years old, with a mustache. He wore a green uniform with braid at the shoulders and a green hat with gold trim. He wore white gloves. Double glass doors opened onto the lobby. The lobby had six easy chairs covered in a tweed wool and two couches of gray leather. The chandelier was crystal and had seven bulbs of approximately 100 watts each.

I won't bore you with any more of this, but I suggested, as I told him to look for other employment, that he might consider becoming a scriptwriter, a clothing designer, or an interior decorator.

There was much more of the report, but it never got around to stating the address, the license plate numbers of cars parked around him, or the fact that he never saw our subject.

So be accurate but not verbose. For example, give the time to the nearest five minutes. No two watches are exactly alike, so it isn't necessary to say "at precisely 9:23 A.M." In fact, that kind of pickiness can cause you problems if you're inconsistent. Note the name and model of a car if you can, but the license number is more important than either of those two facts. In describing people and clothing, a general description is sufficient: "He wore a blue suit and tie, a hat, and was approximately six feet tall."

As Joe Friday used to say on the old "Dragnet" series, "Just give me the facts." The facts are always sufficient.

These next three points are not really guidelines, but they are things that you should keep in mind when you work as your own private investigator.

The first and most important is:

Fictional private eyes are not real. Most of our images and impressions of private investigators and the way they conduct their business are derived from television, the movies, and mystery novels. Mike Hammer, Philip Marlowe, and Sam Spade talk tough, smoke Camels, drink rye, make love, brawl, chase bad guys, and shoot their way through their cases with casual abandon. Rarely do they wear out a pair of shoes—my single biggest expense. Unfortunately, most of what we see and read about private eyes barely resembles the truth. Therefore, the first thing you must do is forget the image you have of the hard-bitten private eye with the quick gun. That person only exists in the imaginations of mystery writers.

What's interesting is that instead of television and the movies imitating real private eyes, real private eyes often imitate television and the movies. A few years back, when "Kojak" was so popular on television, many of the private eyes I knew were sucking lollipops. I'd go to meetings of the local investigators' association and instead of finding a bunch of tough, professional guys, I'd find a bunch of guys with suckers in their mouths calling everybody "Baby." It was disgusting.

But back to the private eyes of fiction. You'll easily recall the scene in the movies: The camera shows us a rundown building in a seedy industrial neighborhood. As we move up the dark stairs we find a dark hallway lined with doors with opaque glass and gold lettering. One of the doors swings open and we see the interior of the private eye's office. He sits at a large wooden desk strewn with newspapers, paper coffee cups, an opened bottle of bourbon, and assorted other junk. There is a dart board on the wall. He's wearing what used to be a white shirt with the sleeves rolled up and a fedora pushed back on his head. His tie is loose and there is a gun in his shoulder holster. His feet are on the desk top and he's casually throwing darts. He appears hung over. Over his shoulder we see his name painted on a dirty window, the sun reflecting it backward and upside down on the floor.

As the scene opens there is a knock on the door. In walks a statuesque blonde showing plenty of cleavage, not to mention a lot of leg. She sits on the edge of the desk, pulls a cigarette from her purse, lights up, and tells her story.

When she finishes, he tells her that it will cost fifty dollars a day plus expenses and they leave arm in arm for lunch as his loyal secretary looks on with envy.

Here is the scene in reality: The investigator's office is located on the tenth floor of an office building in a business area. Inside there are several desks where investigators are at work typing reports and talking on the phone. The investigator is in his private office preparing his court testimony for one of his clients. His secretary welcomes the visitor and then ushers him or her into a tastefully furnished private office, much like that of a lawyer. The investigator is wearing a neat suit and tie, he wears no gun, and his license is hanging on the wall. There is no dart board. The investigator stands to greet the guest. They sit, the potential client in a leather armchair and the investigator behind a glass table that serves as a desk. Case files are neatly stacked to one side. They talk. As they conclude the discussion, the investigator tells the client that his fee will be thirty-five to sixty dollars an hour plus expenses. The client leaves, and the investigator goes back to work.

There are no chases. Again, the scene in fiction: The subject spots the private eye and begins to run. The PI whips his automatic out of his shoulder holster and chases his suspect through back alleys, over fences, and up a fire escape. World-class sprinters could not keep up the pace. When they reach the roof they have a vicious, five-minute fistfight with blows that would have floored Muhammad Ali. The suspect breaks away, and a gunfight erupts. Bullets whiz in every direction, but no one is hit. Somehow they make their way back to the street by dashing through apartment hallways, stopping to fire a few shots on every landing.

Once back on the street they jump in conveniently parked cars and begin a car chase on a crowded expressway. They bang into each other for miles as other drivers swerve and crash to get out of the way. Then, the suspect loses control of his car and crashes into an embankment. The PI rushes up to the car and subdues the injured suspect and carts him off to the police precinct. After a half hour of high-energy action, it's all over and we see the PI having a drink with his girlfriend.

The scene in reality: After several days of careful investigation, which includes extensive research in court records, two dozen or more telephone calls, and seventy-two hours of surveillance, the investigator writes his report and meets with his client to discuss the results of his efforts. No high speed car rides, no fights, no gunplay, only conscientious application of the principles of the business. Not quite as exciting maybe but much more rewarding for the client and much less demanding and dangerous for the PI.

The beautiful women visit other PIs. Finally, there is one other major difference between reality and fiction in the world of the private investigator. Those remarkable female specimens, the ones with the sensational bodies and sparkling teeth, those with all assets and no liabilities, don't usually wander into the office of Irwin Blye. Maybe they just don't have my telephone number. Maybe I need a bigger ad in the yellow pages. Maybe I need a breath mint. At any rate, in my practice, these damsels in distress are few and far between. For me, they too are the stuff of movies and television.

I could give you a hundred examples, but one will be more than sufficient to illustrate what I'm talking about.

A woman in her late sixties came to my office because she felt she had a negligence suit against her landlord. Some six months before, she had stumbled over a loose board in the floor of her apartment, fallen, and broken her hip.

"It's all right now," she told me, "but I have a terrible scar from the operation." We talked a bit more and she explained the whole story to me in detail that was much too detailed. Words like incisions, draining, physical therapy, hips, buttocks, thighs, and more crept into the conversation. Then she launched into a stitch by stitch description of her scar. Finally, she stood up, pulled up her skirt, and showed me her scar in vivid purple. For professional reasons I was forced to look.

I nodded and said, "Thank you," but she kept her skirt hiked up. I said, "Thank you" again but it didn't help. Finally, I said firmly, "That's enough," and she sat down. This was one of the few female thrills I've ever had in the office.

Out of the office there have been exceptions. It has been slightly more exciting from time to time. There was the surveillance that turned into a confrontation between the subject of the surveillance and me, and she happened to be naked at the time. It happened this way. I knocked on the door of the apartment where she was supposed to be meeting her lover. I must have interrupted something interesting because she answered the door with a sheet wrapped around her. Beyond the door I could see a man desperately trying to pull on his pants. I had all I needed, but as I turned to leave she grabbed me by the sleeve and said, "Don't you just wish you were him?" And with that she dropped the sheet on the floor.

In another case I was hired by a wealthy businessman because his daughter felt she was being harassed by a young man she insisted on calling her "boyfriend." I met the father, mother, and daughter (who was quite attractive) at their home in Connecticut. The mother told me that she was certain the young man in question was listening to the daughter's telephone conversations in some mysterious way because he always showed up at the same social events as the daughter. It seemed to me that a girl and her boyfriend should be at these events together anyway, but that didn't seem to be the case here.

Then, though I never figured out what the two things had to do with each other, the mother showed me some photos from a magazine that specializes in pictures of naked women. She pointed to a girl in one particular picture, who she said was her daughter. To say that the scene in the photo was graphic would be an understatement, but to say that it was the daughter would be an overstatement because there was no face visible among all the body parts in that picture.

I pointed out this fact and the mother said she'd prove her point. She calmly told her daughter to take off her clothes and show the nice investigator that it was, in fact, her body in that photo. She started to comply, and I held up my hand. "That won't be necessary," I said. "I will take your word for it." I could see that the father was not taking this very well, and I was getting a bit uneasy myself.

I voiced my doubts as diplomatically as I could, but the mother asked me to at least check into the background of the young man to see why he would be behaving so peculiarly. I agreed, and as I was leaving the father pulled me off to the side and told me, "I want you to go ahead, but I'm sure there's nothing to any of this." He shook my hand and added, "It will make my wife happy, and I want her to be satisfied."

The background check on the young man revealed only that he was a terrific kid. He had gone to a good college, had a good job, had nice parents and good friends. He drank beer on Fridays with his buddies, and he led a perfectly normal, even exemplary, life. I thought the whole thing was the mother's, and possibly the daughter's, imagination.

My report was ready to be mailed when I got a call from the mother asking for another meeting, this time at her husband's office. I showed up and went through what was a virtual repeat of the first encounter even down to the mother telling the daughter to take off her clothes. I looked at the father and saw that he was trying to ignore it all. The daughter was preparing to strip, and again I said, "Hold it."

I opened my briefcase and took out my report. I laid it on the desk and said, "My investigation is closed. The young man is a fine person. I hope my son turns out as well. I suppose I could go on taking your money and continue investigating, but I don't operate that way. Furthermore, though I think your daughter is pretty, I'm not really interested in seeing her nude."

As I left that office, I had to marvel at my aplomb, my professional skill, my unbelievable self-righteousness, and I still wonder from time to time if that was the daughter in those pictures.

These occurrences, rare though they may be, have me looking forward to that warm summer afternoon when Kathleen Turner sweeps into my office wearing a gauzy frock and asks me to spend a few months acting as her bodyguard. Until then, I repeat, the other PIs get the girls.

I've now given you the commandments I live by in my business. Let's move on to some more of the basics.

4

How to Talk to People: Use Your Eyes, Your Ears, Then Your Mouth

When we were kids growing up in the Bronx, we used to play at talking tough. We picked up most of our basic vocabulary on the street, and we got our manner of delivery from the movie tough guys of those days—George Raft, James Cagney, and Richard Widmark—so most of what we said came out of the sides of our mouths. We had several expressions (most of them unprintable) that could only come from growing up on the streets in the Bronx or Brooklyn, and two of my favorites were "Give it t'me or I'll make your face drip blood," and "Don't say nuttin' about my sis-tah or I'll kill ya." Those two expressions seemed to handle most situations where tough talk was needed. In other words, they got results.

I'm going to talk a lot about ways of talking to people in this chapter (and I'm also going to talk about more than talking), but before we begin our little chat, I want to pass on a few words about attitude, that is, your mental attitude when you talk to people. If you're a baseball fan you know that managers always say pitching is 90 percent of baseball. Well, to me, attitude is 90 percent of the talking game. I don't care who you are. If you talk like a wimp, if you're easily intimidated, deterred, put off, then you're going to get nowhere. The guy who's six-foot-six and weighs 260 isn't going to get the time of day if he asks for it like a wimp. On the other hand, the five-foot-one woman who weighs 97 pounds can get the entire Rolodex if she approaches her subject with the right attitude and is assertive. But attitude isn't expressed only by tone of voice. It embraces your posture, the set of your shoulders and head, the firmness of your walk, in short, the way you carry yourself. It also includes the way you dress, and the way you react to the person with whom you're talking. I'll say more about this later, but for now keep in mind that your attitude can be, and often is, the key to success in a conversation and in an entire investigation.

First, however, let's make a general review of the different ways we talk to people, especially when we want to get some information.

I think most people's first inclination is to *ask* for whatever they want in a polite tone and in a gentle manner. Then, if that doesn't work, we switch into a somewhat stronger mode, and we *request* that people do things for us. Failing those two moderate approaches, and depending on how badly we want whatever it is, we can demand, cajole, plead, beg, scream, curse, even joke, in order to get our point across. We can be direct, or indirect. We can be saccharine sweet or acidly bitter. We can be weak and submissive or aggressive and threatening. We can be obsequious and fawning or intimidating and demanding. We can be cool and nice or hot and mean. I have even tried these approaches in combination, sort of a soft-hard-soft-hard-soft approach. They all work under the right circumstances.

Now, what do these different approaches sound like in real life? Here are some examples that I've built around one of my favorite topics—food:

Polite: Miss, would you please bring me the blue plate special? Thank you very much.

Request: I want the blue plate special today. That will be all.

Indirect: It's a nice day, isn't it, and by the way could I get the blue plate special?

Cajole: Do you think that I could induce you to bring me the blue plate special?

Saccharine: Please dear, when you have time, be so kind as to bring me the blue plate special, you sweet thing.

Plead: I've tried everything else, now I'm pleading with you to bring me the blue plate special.

Beg: For God's sake, please have mercy on a poor widower and bring him the blue plate special.

Scream: I ORDERED THE BLUE PLATE SPECIAL AND I WANT IT RIGHT NOW, AND I MEAN NOW!

Curse: Bring me the God damn blue plate special or I'll make your face drip blood.

Intimidate: If you don't take care of my blue plate special, you'll be the blue plate special.

Joke: Did you hear the one about the blue plate special? It seems these two clergymen . . .

Acid: Do you think that you can work it into your busy schedule to bring me the blue plate special I ordered last week?

Mean: If you don't bring me the blue plate special I'll say somethin' unspeakably nasty about ya sistah.

But let me confess, after trying all of these methods over the years, I've determined that polite, polite, and more polite is almost always the winning ticket. What's that old saying, "You get more with honey than with vinegar"? Believe me, in my experience it's true.

It seems that those simple words our parents taught us when we were young, "please," "may I," "appreciate," and "thanks," are still the keys to cooperation. I don't care if you're talking to the president of a bank or the clerk at the supermarket, these are the words that pay dividends and get the groceries delivered. Why? Because most of us are basically softies. We have enough aggression in our daily lives, and when a person is nice we tend to respond in kind. That's what makes con men so successful. They are such nice guys that you can hardly wait to give them your life savings to buy that piece of desert in Arizona or support that wonderful organization that is fighting for the rights of parakeets.

But being polite is also the best policy for another reason. If you're looking for information and you offend the person who can provide it, that person is going to clam up immediately. And don't forget for a minute that *you need what they have* and you aren't going to get it if they don't want you to have it. So, don't offend unless you feel it's absolutely necessary—and even then think twice about it.

Here's a real-life example of what I'm talking about. Not long ago one of my female investigators needed some information from the county courthouse in a small town on Long Island not far from our office. Sherry is an outgoing and attractive person who normally wouldn't raise anyone's hackles, but this day she met up with one of those bureaucrats who had either just had a fight with his wife, had a bad hangover, had gotten up on the wrong side of bed, or was genuinely a bastard.

Whatever the case, she came back to the office complaining of his rudeness (though she did get what she wanted) and when she complains you know she has a case. Here is the story as she told it to me.

She walked into the records room, went to the desk, and told the clerk, "I'd like to see the file on John Dillinger, please."

"What do you want it for?" he responded in tones bespeaking aggravation, bad manners, and irritation at having to respond to a question from the public.

"I need it for a case I'm working on," Sherry replied calmly.

"I'm too busy right now," he said. This time his tone bespoke more than bad manners, it carried obvious anger.

Trying to remain cool, Sherry said, "I know that I'm entitled to see that file, so please let me see it."

"Not right now," he said and stomped away from the counter.

"Just a minute," Sherry called to him firmly, "I'd like to tell you something." And apparently her voice was sufficiently demanding to grab his attention.

"Yeah, what is it?" he said gruffly as he started back toward the counter.

"I came here for your help," she began. "I realize this may be a bad day or a bad time for you but I have my own problems." She noticed that he was listening. "I still have a job to do," she continued, "and to do it I need your help. Your courtesy wouldn't hurt either. Now, if I don't get both of those things I'll find someone in this office who will do this job for me and do it courteously as well." She said all of this without raising her voice but she said it firmly.

By the time she had finished, the clerk was as meek as a lamb. He confessed he had a splitting headache and she sympathized with him, even offered him some aspirin. He may have really had a headache but more than that, he didn't want Sherry to go over his head, which would have caused a considerably more painful ache. Since he didn't seem to her to be a genuine bastard, he probably realized he was wrong anyway. Besides, and very important here, she was asking for his personal help. When she did that his attitude disappeared and he has been so helpful ever since that Sherry sent a note to his supervisor expressing her thanks for the clerk's and the department's invaluable services. The last time Sherry had to go to that courthouse the clerk gave her a cup of coffee and a doughnut.

I tell this story as an illustration of the kind of help and cooperation you can get, even from negative people, if you hang in there and keep your wits (and your temper) about you. We all know how maddening these situations can be and it is often more difficult to maintain your composure than to spout off. I personally have a rather short fuse; consequently I admire people who remain cool and collected under pressure. But I know from experience that it just doesn't pay to fly into a rage because in the end, you are still going to need the same information and the same person you yelled at is most likely the one you'll be depending on to get it for you. How much help would *you* give someone who just yelled in your face?

In most of the situations we're going to be talking about, you will be communicating with people in one of two ways—in person or on the telephone. (Most written communication, mainly filling in and sending forms, will be done without personal contact.) Personal and phone communication each have certain advantages and disadvantages. The main difference is that to save time and money, you will more often use the phone to get what you need.

From my experience the advantages of communication in person are:

• Eye contact. You can go a long way with those baby blues focused directly on the person you're talking to, whether you are of the same sex or not; man to man, woman to woman, man to woman are all the same—looking people in the eye usually has a positive effect.

• Personal charm. If you can turn on the charm it will work well in conjunction with eye contact to create an irresistible package.

• Personal appearance. If you look nice, you have a leg up. All the eye contact and personal charm in the world won't have the right impact if you look like a slob; people respond better when you are properly dressed, neat, and well groomed.

• More time to state your case. The telephone often limits time for conversation, especially if you are talking long distance; people are more inclined to give you extra time and put forth extra energy if you're right there in front of them.

• You're harder to refuse. Your personal presence, the fact that you made the effort to come to that office or agency, makes it psychologically harder for the clerk to turn you away.

There are a couple of disadvantages, however, to in-person communication. If you are the kind of person who gets visibly nervous when dealing with strangers, you diminish your chance of success a bit. Furthermore, you won't be able to consult notes or even read a prepared speech as you could if you were doing the work over the phone.

The advantages of communication by telephone:

• Anonymity. This is one of the real advantages of the phone. You have the choice of identifying yourself or using any name you want and no one will be the wiser. You can always hang up and forget the whole thing without repercussions.

• No visible nervousness. Since the person on the other end of the phone can't see your hands shaking and your eyes wandering around, they won't have the slightest idea that you're nervous.

• Chance to speak from notes. You can use extensive notes, even read a prepared speech if you want, and the person at the other end will think you're a genius with a great command of the language.

• Voice. If you have an exceptionally good speaking voice, the telephone is the place where it is useful. Dulcet tones, a chuckle in the right place, a peel of laughter, a groan of empathy, are all valuable tools you can use to great effect.

The disadvantages of communication by telephone are obvious. You have no chance to make that valuable eye contact or to exploit your appearance. What's more, you'll probably have less time to make your case and the person may simply hang up on you.

Let's take a look at how a face-to-face interview works. I'll use an interview at a bank to illustrate.

I know you're saying to yourself: "A bank, for God's sake! I can't get anything from a bank. Do you expect me to go into a bank and ask for the balance in my husband's checking account? They'll throw me out on my ear. Banks are regulated by the federal government anyway. There's no way."

Let me assure you, there is more than one way. But first you have to dispose of the attitude that a bank is different from any other kind of business enterprise. Banks would like you to think they're different, but they aren't. In fact, they are probably more vulnerable, when it comes to providing information, than the neighborhood gas station. The people who work in a bank are not special. They're regular people just like you. They work for a salary (that is probably lower than your own salary) just like you, and they are anxious to leave at the end of the day, just like you. This is true not only of banks but also of virtually every other large business. Workers don't want trouble from customers or superiors. They put in their eight hours and call it a day. They don't want to make or receive waves. Keep these factors in mind.

Now, let's say that you are filing for divorce and you want to find out everything you can about your husband's assets. You already know where he does his primary banking (there may be other accounts in other banks and you'll have to go through the same process in those banks), so your first stop is "his bank."

Dress properly for the occasion. In other words, don't wear dirty blue jeans and a T-shirt, a formal ball gown, or a very sexy outfit. Look businesslike, that is, neither too dressy nor too casual.

Incidentally, dressing properly is a rule that always applies in private investigation. You should dress for the climate, so to speak.

Look as if you belong where you are. You'll see the relevance of this more clearly in the chapter on surveillance.

To digress a moment, I once had a case that involved a building superintendent, a man whose interests ran from Shakespeare and modern linguistics to oil burners and toilet bowls. When I interviewed him in his apartment to get his pretrial statement as a witness in an accident case, he was dressed for his job—overalls, a baseball cap, heavy shoes. But he was charming and urbane and before I took his statement we sipped wine and discussed the paucity of good fiction from American writers. At the trial he showed up dressed like the leading man in a Noel Coward play. He had on an expensive suit, a tasteful and costly tie, and highly polished designer shoes. He answered all the questions put to him directly and with the speech of an educated man. The problem was, the jury didn't believe a word he said. They had expected a building superintendent more like the man I'd seen out of the courtroom. I think they would have accepted his cultivated speech if he hadn't been so well dressed. To those twelve men and women, he was not credible. That's what I mean about dressing for the part.

Back to the bank. If you know one of the bank's officers, it will be much easier, but for now let's assume you don't know anyone at this particular branch. When you walk in, take a minute to look around. Note the ages of the bank officers. Are there men and women? Does anyone have what you would call a sympathetic face? If you feel more comfortable with a woman, then choose a woman, but I think a woman should go to a male officer and a male to a female officer. Listen to what is being said and who is being called "sir." In a bank most people will be dressed pretty much alike, so your observation of their clothes won't yield much information—though it will in many other situations.

Now, based on your judgment, your gut feeling, select the officer that you think will be most susceptible to your request. It may be sexist to say it, but exploit your advantages. The best bet in this instance is probably a middle-aged man who will be interested in talking to a woman, a person who could add some flavor to his day. After you have made your selection, wait until that person is free. Then make your move.

I've said it above and I'll say it again right now, *your attitude* is going to be the key. A positive attitude makes all the difference. You have to assume that you've got *right* on your side and the bank has something you want, something you're entitled to have. Don't hesitate to use brains, charm, humor, sex, anger, or even tears if absolutely necessary.

Your job is to enlist this person, this bank officer, in your cause. You may have to tell a good portion of your story, play on sympathies and weaknesses that you recognize, even fib a little here and there. Be crafty without seeming to be. Now go. Just walk up to the officer's desk and follow this scenario:

You: "I'd like to get the balances in my husband's accounts, both checking and savings."

Banker: "I'm sorry but we can't give out that information."

You: "But he's out of town for the rest of the month and we need to have the information so we can make some investments."

Banker: "I'm afraid we can't give out that information without an authorization from your husband."

You: "I told you he was out of town and when I called Mr. Jones in the main office he assured me that I'd have no trouble if I came in and gave you some identification."

Banker: "Well, all right then. Could I see some identification? Your driver's license or a credit card will do. Oh, and I'll need your husband's Social Security number."

You: "I have that all right in my purse. Here you are."

If you want additional information about your husband's other banking transactions—outstanding loans, liens or garnishees on his accounts, overdraft privileges, safety deposit boxes—you can ask for it at the same time. I practically guarantee that you will get everything you ask for. In the first place, it is a rare bank officer who isn't subject to the use of a name, real or fictional, from the main office. You may or may not have called someone in authority but it's immaterial. If you say you have made the call that will be enough. The use of a name shows that you have done some checking beforehand. He will assume, therefore, that you "must" know what you're talking about. Second, if you present yourself as a person *entitled to know*, the officer really has very little choice. He or she doesn't want to make waves, and you are obviously a person who could make those waves if you wanted to.

When you've finished, thank the person sufficiently, use his name, and make your exit. You will undoubtedly feel excited with your accomplishment and you should. The barrier is now broken and you can return to that same person time and again if necessary, even get information over the phone.

One of the ways we talk to people involves knowing the jargon, the right words to use in the situation. It's often as simple as asking for the right number on an official form or dropping the right phrase at the right time. For example, when I'm on a street surveillance, sitting for hours in a parked car or hanging out in front of a building leaning against a lamppost, I am pretty inconspicuous to the average person because most people don't pay that much attention to strangers on the street. But a policeman, either in a car or on foot, will eventually notice me. At that point he may ask me what I'm doing holding up the side of the building for an hour. I can either say, "I'm waiting for my girlfriend," which certainly could be the truth, but there is a standard answer: "I'm on the job. It's private." This is the signal to him that I'm not just some loitering sex maniac—I've often felt my PI license gives me only one privilege and that's to loiter—and he won't bother me again. If I'm still there after the police change shifts I may have to repeat the process, but it is a recognized method of identification.

Of course there are an almost infinite number of potential situations and an infinite number of ways to talk and terms to use when talking to people and we can't possibly cover them all here. But some of the other jargon you'll find useful (and entertaining) can be found in the PI lexicon in the back of the book.

THE FIRST LINE OF DEFENSE

How many times have you called a company or a government agency hoping to get some basic information, absolutely public information, only to run into the following roadblock:

Them: "Good morning, Sprockets, Incorporated."
  You: "Hello, could you tell me where I can get some information about your company?"

Them: "I'm sorry, you have to talk to the promotion department to get that information."

You: "Thank you. Will you please transfer my call to that department."

Them: "I'm sorry but you have to call them directly."

You: "All right. Please give me their number."

Them: "I'm sorry you'll have to get that information from the promotion department."

This is pretty close to the classic catch-22. It is a perfect example of what I like to call the "first line of defense," a successful strategy of Sprockets, Incorporated, banks, insurance companies, major corporations, and government agencies at all levels. It's a strategy that was developed to withhold, obscure, obfuscate, and otherwise prevent you from getting information, even (maybe especially) information you are absolutely entitled to have.

In war, the job of the soldiers who are on this first line of defense is to prevent the enemy from breaking through to the troops that are behind the lines doing all that behind-the-lines work, which includes manning the inner defenses, doing paperwork, picking up cigarette butts, and drinking beer at the post PX. The trench soldiers are mostly privates, and they have two types of authority—little and none. There may be a few sergeants in their ranks to give them orders and moral support, and possibly a lieutenant who tells the sergeants what to do, but even these low-ranking officers have little real authority.

Well, in many businesses and government agencies the lines of defense and authority are the same. It's like a little war, but in this case only sensibilities get injured. The people who man the first line of defense in these places—mostly privates, with a sergeant or two—are the ones who answer the phones and try to prevent the enemy (in this case the public) from talking to anyone behind the front lines.

These are the people who answer that general phone number listed in the phone directory. It's the number you call first because it's the only number you have available. This number, usually called "Customer Service" or "Customer Relations," is generally something like 123-4000. Depending on the size of the organization, there may be five, ten, or fifty privates who pick up the call when that number is dialed.

What is their job? To give the bare minimum of information necessary to fend off the enemy. They have no authority and may, in fact, be told, "Never refer a caller to another number in the company." In reality, this practice does discourage most callers. Those few people who demand to speak to someone else are referred to the sergeant on duty, and that is most likely the end of the trail. We've all had it happen, the disembodied voice that says, "I'm sorry sir, but that's all the information I have." And the operator isn't lying. These people have so little information they can't possibly reveal much. This method is successful because it is very discouraging to have to work so hard for something that should be so easy.

Now I'm going to let you in on the private investigator's top-secret method for getting around this first line of defense, for flanking this thin line of trench soldiers, and plunging into the vulnerable underbelly of the organization. It's so simple that you're going to say to yourself, "You don't have to be a private eye to figure that one out." I can only say the Pythagorean theorem was simple after Pythagoras worked it out.

It's obvious that these companies and government agencies have more than one number. They use one general number for outsiders, but that number is only indicative of all the phone numbers in that company. After all, there is a phone on virtually every desk, and most of them are extensions of the main number. so, using the example above, all you have to do is dial 123-4001 or 123-4090 or 123-4110, depending on the size of the company, and you've bypassed customer service, and in the process you've bypassed the first line of defense.

Almost any other number that follows the main number by a hundred or two will put you deep inside the company, able to attack by surprise. Why is a company like General Motors or the United States government vulnerable at this level? Again, it's simple. It's because the person picking up the phone deep inside the company normally doesn't get calls from the outside and is not prepared to hear the voice of the public on the other end of the line.

When the phone rings on that desk on level four, aisle two,

column nine, desk six, the person answering automatically thinks that it is either the boss, a friend, or a lover because they are the only people who know that extension. But surprise. It isn't any of those people. It's you, the public. And you have instantly achieved the advantage of surprise plus the additional advantage of being thought of as an "insider" because only an insider could possibly know that particular number. At that point, if you say, "I'm looking for loan information on a Mr. Jack McSmedley," they'll say, "Sure, what can I do for you?" They usually won't even ask your name. They certainly don't know who you are, but since you have the number you must be legitimate.

Having inside information of any kind immediately puts you in the other fellow's camp and that's exactly where you want to be. That's one of the reasons I follow the newspapers so closely. I like to file away facts that may be useful someday. For example, not long ago I read that AT&T was laying off some of their long-lines workers. I put that in my memory bank because I knew that I would have to talk to someone at the telephone company sooner or later and I would be able to drop that little piece of information into the conversation. Then I can bitch with them a little about the problems of labor and management and sympathize with them in general by telling them that my brother-in-law was just about to get his pink slip from the company out in Ohio. It's only a little thing, but it establishes rapport, instills confidence, and opens the floodgates of information.

Now, what do you say when you get through to this desk behind the enemy lines? You have to know what question to ask; otherwise you lose the advantage. So say something like this:

Jack: "Jack Jones."
You: "Jack, this is Clark Kent. I'm trying to find out the price of coffee in Brazil."
Jack: "I'm sorry, but you've got the wrong extension. That number is 3245. Just dial 123-3245 and ask for Shirley Smith. Or if you want, I'll try and transfer the call for you."
You: "Thanks. Yeah, try and transfer me."

You have the element of surprise—be nimble and quick. You have the psychological advantage because Jack Jones thinks this may be important. And if you say, "I just spoke to the manager of customer service," or "I'm calling from Mr. Blah's office," the red carpet will be laid out.

Now you're on the right track and though you'll probably be cut off when Jack tries to transfer the call (it happens all the time), you'll still have the proper extension, the name of the person you need to talk to, and the name of the person who answered the phone, which you can use for reference. You can use those two names inside the company until you get others.

When you finally get the extension you want, you need only say:

You: "Is this Shirley Smith?"
She: "Yes, it is. Can I help you?"
You: "Yes, you can. Jack Jones gave me your extension."

The door is now flapping wide open. Of course, now you have to be smart enough and prepared enough to continue to ask the right questions to keep the door and the conversation open.

WHAT TO DO WHEN THEY SAY "NO"

In my office we have a motto that we live by, and if I ever get around to it I'm going to have a big banner hung on the wall that says, Don't Take No for an Answer. The word "no" is an extremely difficult word for most people to handle. Most people have this idea in their heads that no actually means no. But that may not be, and usually is not, the case.

Remember having this conversation with your parents when you were a little kid?

You: "Mom, can I get a Red Ryder air rifle for Christmas?"
Mom: "No, absolutely not. You'll shoot out somebody's eye with one of those things."
You: "Please, Mom."
Mom: "I said no, and I mean no. You could shoot your own eye out."
You: "Please."

Mom: "I told you no."
 You: "Why?"
Mom: "I told you why."
 You: "Why?"
Mom: "Because."
 You: "Because why?"
Mom: "Just because."
 You: "Aw, Mom, please."
Mom: "Well, maybe."
 You: "Does maybe mean yes?"

We always knew that when our parents said no to something, the chances were good they really meant maybe. We also knew that if we could get them to say maybe then it would be very easy to push them into saying yes.

I don't know why we forget this when we get to be adults, because it's an effective means of getting information. "No," more often than not, is the first word you'll hear. It doesn't make any difference if you're trying to find Cheddar cheese in the grocery store or the last known heir to an estate. People say no. They are used to saying it, they may even like to say it, but they say it primarily because it's easier. It means that they won't have to do any additional work.

Let me give you a simple example. Say you go into a department store to buy a pair of blue jeans. You look around for a bit, and you find what you're looking for but not in your size. You approach the salesperson and ask if the store has these particular jeans in your size. The immediate answer is almost always, "No, only what you see," and the implication is often, "And how can you be so dumb." Now, common sense tells you that this store or any other department store has plenty of jeans in size thirty-two, so why is this person telling you there aren't any? It's most likely because he doesn't want to go to the stockroom and get them for you. Obviously, if you want the jeans you have to pursue the issue and that takes undue energy on your part, so you may just forget it. This is why "no" usually works.

When you're looking for information, you have to ask yourself: Do they mean no, they don't have the information, or no, I can't have it. To find out the answer you have to ask the question another way. But first, make sure the person understands what it is you're looking for. There is often misunderstanding in oral (and written) communication, so take the time to clarify your request and try not to sound too bitchy about it. At the same time, try to figure out who you're talking to. Is it the lowliest person in the chain of command or has that person been around for a while? Is it an experienced person who has real authority? Does the person need approval of what he does or is he a supervisor, or even the boss? Keep in mind the limitations of the person you're talking to.

If the answer is "Yes, we have the information, but I can't give it to you," then your job is to persuade that person that he should give you the information in question. You have to motivate that person, and you can use any one of a number of methods, including those mentioned in the earlier part of this chapter.

Just remember that "no" is not necessarily the end of your inquiry. Keep the person engaged. Rephrase your question. You may have asked the equivalent of, "Is the sky cloudy today?" and the person said, "No." Now ask, "Is the sky blue today?" That's not the same question. They may say, "Yes, it is," and at that point you begin to get information.

I've often felt that acquiring information over the phone from adults is a lot like talking to little children over the phone. Not much information is volunteered. If you ask a child, "Is your mommy around?" the child may say no even though Mommy is in the next room, because she isn't "around." "Did anyone call?" is another question that a child will answer with a no. If you then ask, "Did Frank call?" you can get a yes because Frank is a specific person, not "anyone." Therefore it's important to ask precisely the right question. People will only put out up to the limits of their job responsibility. They are told to answer the phone and answer a question and hang up, and that's what they are paid to do. But with perseverance you can get them to do more.

When I'm not making any progress or I realize that the door is about to be closed, I often try to create a sense of confusion at the other end of the line. It works much better on the telephone than in person, by the way. I'll bring up something entirely extraneous to our conversation. I may start the confusion by saying something like this: "Was I calling about the account of John Smith? I don't remember now. Could you tell me what you have on him?" Then, as soon as that is out of my mouth, I'll say something unrelated like: "My daughter got married last Sunday, and it was wonderful." If the person was about to ask me who I am or why I want the information, this diverts him and takes his mind off his own question. You have to pick these spots carefully, but the worst thing that can happen is that he eventually hangs up.

Use your head, pick your spots, and dart into every opening. If you're talking to someone with the sniffles or a cough, you can say, "It sounds like you have a cold. There is a lot of that going around." Ask about them. Don't hesitate to get personal.

And then there's humor. I love it. Humor is often the thing that finally breaks through the toughest veneer though you have to be a bit careful because a misplaced remark, the wrong subject matter, or a punch line that offends, can end a conversation in a hurry. What I like to do is make up my mind that I'm going to make the person to whom I'm talking at least smile. Making them laugh may be out of the question. When I produce that smile, the chances of my success are much greater. There are very few people who are impervious to the good-natured approach. It's not that I start telling jokes. Instead, I create a lightness in my voice, a tone that is nonthreatening, and I'll make a remark that indicates I'm human and I know they're human. You can't prepare a comedy routine, but you can have a small stock of quips about the weather, the current news, or television, because virtually everyone recognizes the inherent humor in these facets of our daily lives. Be careful to use humor only when it seems appropriate. Use it, but don't abuse it.

Commiseration is another successful method of breaking through in a difficult conversation. If the person seems to want to bitch about the vagaries of his job or the weather or life in general, you can commiserate and bitch with him, but be sure to agree basically with whatever he has to say. If he says, "The government's policies are putting people out of work," and you don't think that's the case, don't get on your progovernment soapbox. You can answer in an equivocal way by saying, "Yes, that's certainly true for some people.'' This doesn't antagonize your contact, and it doesn't compromise your principles because what you're saying is true.

In this kind of situation I always think of the story of the famous old stage actress who was making a comeback on Broadway. After the show on opening night, she was met backstage by her old friends and she asked one of them how she had liked her performance. It had been a disaster, and everyone but the actress herself knew it. Not wanting to hurt the old girl's feelings, her friend hesitated for a moment and then said, with her feet planted firmly in midair, ''My dear, how do you do it?'' But she was off the hook.

Now, whether I've gotten what I needed or not, I always take one final step. I ask the person I'm talking to what they think my next move should be. ''If you were me,'' I ask, ''where would you look next?'' This puts them in your camp. They may not budge very far for you, but every inch helps. If they are hesitant you can say, ''Is there anyone else in your office or a branch office somewhere I should talk to?'' Again, you have given them the opportunity to pass the buck, and if you've been persuasive they will pass it.

Are you lowering yourself to do some of these things? Possibly. Will it help? Probably. Is it worth it to get what you want? Absolutely.

5

Divorce and Other
Matters Matrimonial

SPECIAL NOTE:
Please handle this chapter with extreme care.

The reason for this warning is simple. My matrimonial work includes suits for divorce, separations, child custody, and plain old-fashioned adultery, and these situations and their variations have one thing in common—*they are all highly emotional.*

We all know that even the most stable marriages can become volatile from time to time. Partners will become irritated, accusations will be made, tempers will flare, voices will be raised.

Unstable marriages are many times more volatile than stable ones. If you suspect your spouse of having an affair, you are already emotionally wrought up. If you find solid evidence of hanky-panky, your ire increases manyfold. If you confront your partner about the matter, crockery may fly. If you see "those two" together your eyes will be filled with molten lava and your tongue will spit fire. Emotions, my friend.

Any law enforcement officer will tell you that the call he or she dreads the most is the summons to break up a domestic dispute. Because emotions are running so high in these situations, the potential for violence is tremendous, and the cop is usually caught in the middle and put in a position of not being able to do anything to mollify either party. It's a fact that police officers suffer more injuries while on calls that involve domestic situations than on any other type of emergency call.

In matrimonial squabbles emotions build, then increase geometrically, and finally someone explodes. The cops are called by a neighbor, someone grabs a knife, the knife strikes flesh, blood flows onto the kitchen floor, warrants are issued, and people are carted off to the precinct house and sometimes the hospital.

So be warned. The situations discussed in this chapter are emotionally charged. If you decide to do your own matrimonial investigation you will obviously have to be intimately involved every step of the way. It cannot be otherwise. As a disinterested or neutral third party, I've witnessed the emotional tidal wave that develops, builds, and finally crashes on the parties involved in matrimonial suits hundreds of times. Even as a professional, it's often hard for me to remain unaffected. If I have developed information that substantiates a case of adultery, I have to tell the party who hired me. That's something like telling a person they have cancer. There is no easy way. As soon as you say, "Mrs. Jones, I'm afraid I have bad news," the tears start to flow. It doesn't make any difference if Mrs. Jones despises the bastard, she is still upset. Men react emotionally, too. More often men scream and yell, but there are usually tears as well.

If you handle your own investigation (or any part of it) there is one thing you must try to do, one rule you can invoke for yourself though it will be difficult. The police call it by various names, but it is most commonly referred to as the "first directive." The first directive is simple—it says, "Don't get emotionally involved." Much easier said than done, I assure you. Nevertheless, I strongly advise you try and obey this directive. Sure, I know you're saying to yourself, "I hate that so-and-so with a passion and I couldn't possibly become emotional about it." Or, "She's stolen my youth and my money and she can rot in hell for all I care." Or, "I'm too emotionally exhausted to care." But after saying any of these things, take a look at what you said. The words "hate" and "so-and-so," "passion," "stolen," "rot in hell," and "emotionally exhausted," are about as highly charged as you can get, and you haven't even started yet.

Now, if you are looking for the clues that indicate matrimonial problems, if you want to know the grounds for divorce and how to establish them, the proven methods are here for your use. Just remember, no one, but no one, wins the mental health award in a matrimonial case.

WHY DO IT YOURSELF?

With the emotional stakes so high, why on earth would a person want to handle his or her own matrimonial investigation?

There are three primary reasons, and I give them in the order of importance.

The first is grounded in sheer need. When you see your married life beginning to fall apart, you will want to get involved just to see for yourself what kind of person your partner really is. You may have a burning desire to catch the two of them making love (or at least find evidence to prove infidelity) and later be able to confront them with dates, times, and other details that would prove, beyond a shadow of a doubt, that you know what's going on. The other side of that coin is that you want to exonerate your partner in the worst way and the only course of action is to investigate the situation like a professional. Instead of hoping to find the two of them making love, you hope to find out for sure that those frequent trips your husband is making to St. Paul are really for business.

The second reason is an extension of the first: revenge. It's a legitimate reason. You feel you've been wronged and you want to make it known that you are the one who is suffering. You want revenge, and you can get it by proving that your suspicions were correct. I think this is the main reason people want to know about infidelity, but my clients tell me that just needing to know the truth, to clear the air and their minds, is the main reason.

The third reason is financial. The average matrimonial investigation conducted by a private investigator costs nearly $4,000. That is a lot of money to spend finding grounds for divorce when, as an intimate partner in the marriage, you know damn well without spending a cent that something strange is going on even though you can't prove it. Of course, hiring someone can pay big dividends as well. If you spend $4,000 to get a settlement of $250,000 or $500,000, it's clearly worth the investment. On the other hand, you can still get that $250,000 settlement and save at least some of that professional fee by doing a portion of the job yourself.

I've had many naive and self-deceived clients in my time, but I've also had some very astute matrimonial clients. By the time the clever ones get to my office they have in their hands half the facts they need, and a good idea of where to get the rest of them. It's like a doctor friend of mine says, "People who come to my office do at least seventy-five percent of the diagnosis for me. They tell me what hurts and I just have to apply my experience to tell them what is causing the problem." It's much the same with a PI. People with some of the facts help make my job easier.

SOME CASE STUDIES IN EMOTION

Let me give you an assortment of examples of the kind of heavy emotional strain that exists in a matrimonial case, the kinds of pressures people endure, the kinds of pressures that draw a person's strings so taut that they are close to the breaking point. Sometimes they break.

This first example comes from a case I handled years ago. We had been hired by a man to follow his wife because he was sure she was having, in his words, "an affair with a son of a bitch from my office." At his request we followed her for two days and finally traced her to an apartment not far from the office of our client. Sure enough, a few minutes after she entered the building, our client's business associate showed up and went inside. It seemed that, indeed, she was meeting her lover there during the lunch hour—an extended lunch hour, that is.

In order to be less conspicuous and to get a better vantage point, my partner and I stationed ourselves on a roof opposite the apartment building where the couple was meeting. As luck had it in this case, we had a direct view of the apartment and the bedroom and we could see them clearly. As is often the case, they didn't bother to pull the shades.

I say "often the case" because clandestine lovers want to live dangerously. They take chances, they leave clues, they openly flaunt the conventions of society. The chance of discovery actually becomes part of the pleasure, the sexuality, and the challenge of the affair. Hence, open blinds, the hint of lipstick on the collar, a telephone number "accidentally" left on the dresser, the smell of another man's after-shave lotion on the cheek, and even more blatant hints. If I gave you a complete list it could be embarrassing.

At any rate, my partner and I watched them long enough to get the kind of proof we needed—it was clearly not what one would normally call a business lunch—and the next day we reported our findings to the husband.

He was enraged, of course, and he demanded that we take him to the roof two days later (that seemed to be the couple's pattern) so that he could see for himself what his wife was doing with and to his friend. I told him in no uncertain terms I thought it was a bad idea because of the potential for emotional trauma. I told him it would be like going under the knife without anesthesia. But even that simile couldn't deter him and he insisted. He said, among other things, that since he was paying the bill he had a right to come along. So, against my better judgment, we took him to that roof. Again, we caught the couple in the act of making love. As I had feared might happen, the husband, a sensitive man, had a violent reaction and almost instantly became sick to his stomach. For over half an hour he couldn't stop throwing up. As the minutes passed, he was clearly becoming weaker and I was concerned that he might be working himself into a heart attack or a stroke. Finally, during a break in his spasms, we were able to drag him off the roof, and we took him to a nearby hospital emergency room where he was given a sedative.

Based on our evidence, our client went on to sue for divorce and won easily. But the emotional cost of seeing his wife making love to another man had been very high. After the judge made his ruling in the case, the man came to me and apologized.

"I should have known better than to go up on that roof," he said, "or to get involved at all. You were absolutely right. It was a stupid thing for me to do."

"I know," was all I said.

On another case—and I'm telling you about this one with some trepidation—a woman insisted on coming with me on a surveillance I had been keeping on her husband. I knew about his liaison because I had already been tailing him for two weeks. She wanted a divorce badly so she thought it would be very rewarding, and possibly great fun, to catch "the filthy son of a bitch," as she called him, in the act. I advised her, as I would any client, that it wasn't in her best interests to take part in the investigation at this point. But she continued to insist, and I gave in.

I picked her up on that same night and we drove to an apartment complex in a suburban community on Long Island where, on a regular basis, the husband had been meeting his girlfriend. We waited for about half an hour before the husband drove up, parked the car, and went into the apartment. We had an unobstructed view of the living room and bedroom windows (again, no shades, blinds, or drapes were drawn) and we could see them drinking and talking. Then they stood up and began kissing and hugging with some passion.

I could sense that the wife was getting more agitated by the minute, and by the time the couple reached the bedroom, she was beside herself. "I'll get even with that bastard," she kept repeating, among other things not quite so printable. Finally, as if to get even immediately, to get her revenge even though the husband would know nothing about it, she began making sexual advances to me. As she stared at the bedroom window and cursed him, she put her hand on my knee and then started moving it up my leg. I knew that if I didn't do something quickly we were in trouble, so I took the only action I could think of. I reached for the keys with the intention of starting the car and getting out of there. But before I could turn the key in the ignition, her hand was on mine and she yanked the keys out of the ignition and threw them on the floor.

"If you keep doing what you're doing I won't be able to do my job," I said in protest.

"What do you mean," she said furiously. "I'm paying you, and now I'm going to please you. As far as I'm concerned that's part of doing your job for me." Not being Superman, I had no alternative. She pulled me toward her and as her lips met mine I could hear the ocean wind and the waves breaking on the shore. Fade to black.

The next morning she called to say that she had no idea she would become so emotionally wrought up. I reminded her that I had warned her of the dangers involved. "But I really don't care what happens to the guy, and that's the truth," she said in response.

"So much for not caring," I thought to myself.

One more example will serve to solidify my point that there is extreme pressure in all matrimonial situations. In this case, the pressure was too great for my client to handle. She was a lawyer with a large law firm in New York. I met her twice and liked her very much. She was a bright, attractive, reserved person from a wealthy family. During our meetings she sat very stiffly in her chair as she talked to me, she tapped her fingers nervously on her purse, which she kept in her lap, and she often spoke in clipped sentences. After those two meetings with her I felt certain she was holding back her emotions.

She told me that she and her husband had been married for five years, but they hadn't been getting along well for more than a year at that point. She strongly suspected that he was seeing another woman, but she didn't know who, or where he was seeing her. She hired me to find out so that she could begin divorce proceedings. Her story was delivered in a direct lawyerly style and she showed none of the responses I usually see. There wasn't the trace of a tear in her eyes and she never even sniffled.

One weekend not long after that, the husband told her he had to go to Washington on business. He, too, was an attorney and often made trips out of town, and it was on those trips that she felt he was having an affair. She called me and I picked up the surveillance. Instead of driving to the airport, the husband drove to a small town on the New Jersey shore and I followed him. He spent the weekend with a woman, the suspected girlfriend, in a nice seaside hotel. On Monday morning he flew to Washington and returned home on Monday evening to his wife and his apartment in Manhattan.

I gave my client this information and she took it in the stoic manner that seemed to be her style. Though I didn't know it at the time, she was too stoic, too unemotional. She thanked me and said she would be in touch if she needed any further assistance. I heard no more from her, but two weeks later I read in the paper that she had jumped out of her office window and fallen twenty floors to her death. She didn't even leave a note.

Did I say I don't get emotionally involved? That may be hedging a bit. This is not a typical case, but in almost every case someone suffers, and I wonder if there is anything more I might have done to ease that suffering. In this instance I was extremely upset because I felt that surely there was something I could have done to temper the facts, some type of additional help or direction I could have offered the young woman. Maybe reaching out a bit more would have prevented the tragedy.

I know from experience, however, that I had done what I had been hired to do and that there was nothing to be gained by blaming myself for what happened in this case. Still, if . . .

Now that you're fully aware of the potential hazards in matrimonial cases, let's move on to some of the things you should know if you decide to go ahead with your own matrimonial investigation. I don't suppose I've scared you off. At least I hope I haven't.

GROUNDS

In many states, "no-fault" divorces are available, and for this type of divorce no grounds are needed. All two people have to do is agree that they don't want to stay married and the court abides by those wishes (usually after one year), with the property divided between the partners.

If you want to sue for divorce in order to get a greater share of the assets of your mate than a no-fault decision would provide, you will have to prove that you have grounds for that divorce. There are many grounds available, but the most common are adultery, mental cruelty, physical cruelty, abandonment, and mental incompetence.

The most common type of case for me, however, is adultery. In fact, more than 80 percent of my matrimonial cases involve one spouse finding someone else with whom to share a bed for sexual reasons. When a husband has a girlfriend, the wife is angry. When it is the reverse, the husband is usually shocked and confused, especially when the wife has found a younger man.

Some people come to me to get the goods on their partners so they can get a divorce, but others want the evidence in order to try and find out what's gone wrong with the marriage and to fix it. You might find it surprising, but it's about half and half.

The ratio of men to women clients is also about fifty-fifty today. Fifteen years ago my clients were 75 percent women who had reason to believe their husbands were cheating on them. Now the extramarital relations or "cheating ratio," as I like to call it, has reached equilibrium.

Finding grounds for divorce is the primary reason matrimonial clients come to me, but there are others.

• Many people are seeking revenge. They don't necessarily even want a divorce, they only want to assemble the facts that can then be used to batter the partner into senselessness.

• Others simply want to put an end to the gossip and rumor about their relationship. They want to be able to say publicly that there is or isn't something wrong.

• Sometimes a woman dating a married man wants to find out about his wife and if the things the husband is telling her about the wife are really true. I've found the mistress is often a tough adversary, willing to risk a lot to gain a lot.

• On the other side of the coin, men dating married women want to find out about her husband and check out her story about actively seeking a divorce or not having any kids.

The permutations of these themes are interesting and varied to say the least, and when I finish with the investigation business I think I will have credentials to start a new career as a psychologist. Here's an example of a matrimonial case that gave me some of my training as an amateur shrink.

About three years ago I got a call from a woman in Dallas who said she wanted me to help her on a matrimonial matter. On the phone she sounded charming, cultured, and fiftyish. I could not help liking her on the phone. She was so bright and bubbly I could almost see her smiling face.

She was calling me, she said, because she had seen me on the CBS program "60 Minutes" with Dan Rather. She thought that since I was not only a private investigator but seemed to know celebrities (after all, I was on TV), she felt I could be of help.

She told me a long, involved, and convoluted story, but the gist of it was that she had been married to a number of big names in show business at one time or another. She said they were all now denying that she had been married to them, and, unfortunately, she had no marriage certificates to prove her claims.

I asked her if she had ever lived with any of them, and she replied that she had lived with Frank Sinatra, Roy Clark, and several more for up to six months before they split. I told myself immediately that this was crazy, but I have learned that things are not always as they seem. Besides, she sounded completely sane on the phone.

As if to answer my question, she said, "I realize you might think this whole thing is crazy, Mr. Blye, and that I'm out of my mind, but I assure you that I'm not crazy and I'm willing to pay a fee for your services."

"This does seem improbable," I told her, "but if you want, I'll take the case." I figured my way out was to ask for a fee so out of line that she would forget the whole thing. "My fee for this type of investigation," I said, "is a thousand dollars a day, all expenses included." To me that was A FEE. Without the trace of a waver in her voice she said that was fine and agreed to send me some material to work on.

I thought that was certainly the end of it, but about a week later I got a thick envelope of information, a list of her "husbands," and a certified check for my entire fee in advance. There were eighteen names on her list. It was nuts. Here I was with this enormous check in my hand, so I called her, explained that I felt eighteen husbands were about fifteen too many, and said, "I'd like you to reconsider. I'll be glad to return your check." I wasn't particularly pleased with the last part of that statement.

She said graciously, "Thank you for your concern, Mr. Blye. But please proceed with your investigation."

I went to work. I've learned that for everything there is a source. There are reference books, encyclopedias, almanacs, annual reports, lists of organizations, and much more. In this case the source was the Library for the Performing Arts at Lincoln Center. I sent an investigator there to check the official biographies of all the people on the woman's list. He took extensive notes from those biographies, made photocopies of pertinent passages and pictures, and from this we prepared a thick, detailed report. We also phoned the agents and lawyers of a number of people on the list, and we included their statements in that report. What we found was what we expected. She had never been married to any of the men on the list.

I was a little disappointed. She was so pleasant that I wanted to find at least one legitimate marriage for her. I sent a large envelope with this information, and a covering letter explaining our methods, and again, I thought that was the end of it. About two weeks later I got a letter from the lady that I was sure was going to contain at least a portion of the riot act. I was ready for the worst, and I held it at arm's length as I opened it. I had not deposited her check yet, so I was ready to return her fee without any questions if she wanted that. But her letter was so complimentary that I almost blushed. It said in part:

> You're a genius, Mr. Blye. I am so relieved that I wasn't married to all these people. You have lifted a terrible weight from my mind. You have more than earned your fee. Thank you so very much.

Apparently my investigation had not only cleared her conscience but had cleared her imagination as well. This gives you an idea of the exquisite variations that exist in matrimonial matters.

Since adultery is the most common ground used for obtaining a divorce, it will be useful if I explain its various forms. The most common is sexual, that is, your spouse is making love to another person. But there are two other forms of adultery that are also grounds for divorce. One is called "opportunity" and the other is called "inclination." Both can be used to prove a basic case of adultery. Mark well that the burden of proof in all cases lies on the person bringing the charges. And I know you'll find that assuming things and proving things are two quite different matters. Also note: The things I'm telling you here are true in most states. Each state has its own set of laws covering matrimonial issues (and everything else for that matter), but often the variations are slight. Check with a lawyer to make sure of the applicable laws in your state.

"Opportunity," which means exactly what it says, can be easy or difficult to prove, so let's take a closer look. If you can prove that your wife and her friend have gone to a motel or hotel, that is sufficient evidence to establish opportunity. It is valid and conclusive in almost every instance and in almost every state.

You don't have to catch them in the act because it is sufficient that they clearly had the opportunity. Since there is only a remote chance of another valid reason for going to a hotel or motel you have a case. I have often pondered the other reasons why two people enter a motel or hotel room together, and even my vivid imagination can't come up with much. The possibility of completely innocent behavior is remote. I suppose they could be watching the afternoon soaps, planning an office party, or even writing a book, but I doubt it and the courts doubt it, too.

Still, you need to prove that you actually witnessed them entering the place of liaison, so it's imperative that you do one of three things, and preferably all three:

• Have someone with you to corroborate your statements. Corroboration is of utmost importance in matrimonial cases. One person's word is sometimes acceptable, but the word of two witnesses is more than twice as acceptable. This means you'll have to recruit a good friend to accompany you on these excursions.

• Establish the fact that you were there by doing what I do, which is registering at the same motel or hotel yourself. You don't have to stay, but this gives you a written receipt, which is a record of having been where you said you were at the time you said you were there.

• Take down the license numbers of the cars parked in the motel lot. You may never have to use them, but if necessary you can contact people for corroboration. You won't make any friends with this tactic, but it can help your case.

In other nonpublic locations and situations where the opportunity for cohabitation seems probable, things are not so clear-cut, so be careful. The mere fact that a man and woman enter an apartment building together is no proof that they entered a particular apartment together. You may feel certain that they did but that isn't good enough. And if they entered an apartment together it doesn't necessarily mean that they were alone in that apartment though you may feel certain that they were. There could very easily be a third, fourth, or fifth party in that apartment. Since the opportunity for sexual relations is considered to be less likely when a third party is around, you don't have the same case unless you can prove they were in the apartment alone. One way to establish that fact is to place a phone call to the apartment before they enter. If there is no answer the apartment is probably empty (it's a reasonable assumption). No third party is present. Therefore, when they arrive they will be alone in that place. This obviously assumes that you have established the residency or ownership of the apartment in your previous investigation and have obtained the phone number. This isn't as unlikely as it may sound, as you will see a little later in this chapter.

If the couple in question goes to a private house, the situation is much the same. A third party could certainly be present. To establish proof that the couple is alone you can follow the same calling procedure I just mentioned. A private residence does offer the chance to observe one additional thing: If it's after dark and the couple enters a dark house the chances are better that there is no third party involved. At any rate, keep in mind the possibility of a third party.

''Inclination'' simply means that two people have the inclination to commit adultery though they may not have actually done so. It is a somewhat more difficult ground to prove. For example, if you observe the subjects in question in an embrace, kissing on the street corner, holding hands in a restaurant, or otherwise showing extra affection in public, you have a chance to prove inclination. On the other hand, if your mate, for example, is normally openly affectionate or known for regularly having lunch or dinner with other men or women, and you see him or her being affectionate with a stranger, your case is not very strong.

But inclination can lean in the direction of opportunity and when it falls over it becomes opportunity. Here's an example of a situation where both opportunity and inclination were established. I have a friend, a lawyer who looks so much like Dudley Moore I chuckle every time I see him. I had known him for years when he came to see me with tears in his eyes and said, "Louise is seeing another guy on the side, and we separated last week." He asked me to take the case and to help him prove she was having an adulterous relationship. Of course I took it.

Louise was an exceptionally pretty, statuesque woman with a figure that wouldn't stop, and she was about ten years younger than my lawyer friend. As I thought back on his courtship, I remembered that I was surprised by the differences in their size, age, and looks. Then, I was frankly surprised when they got married. Since their marriage I had seen less of them, but when I did see them they seemed very happy indeed. Still, I wasn't particularly surprised when he told me she was having an affair and they were splitting.

He wanted to be part of the surveillance, so both he and I followed her one night to a very expensive restaurant where she met her male friend. Fortunately for us, the couple sat near the window, and we were able to observe them from the car. If they hadn't sat in plain sight, we wouldn't have been able to go in because obviously she would have recognized us. This is one of those cases where I would have called in another operative if necessary. During dinner we could see her clearly. She was kissing and hugging this guy, and he was doing the same. We had a perfect case of inclination.

When they left the restaurant, they went to what we already knew was his house. When we pulled up and parked two houses away, the man's house was pitch black. When he and Louise went inside, lights started showing all over the place. Then, one by one, they went out, and only the light in an upstairs room stayed on.

By this time I had spent more than six hours with "Dudley," and he had been talking my ear off about this guy and his wife and about how much he loved her and hated him and on and on. It was a continuous flow of love and invective, hour after hour. I was getting brutally unhappy with his chatter. Besides I was getting physically tired.

As we sat and watched the house, he said, "Irwin, what do you think they're doing in there?" I was so tired of listening to him that I told him in great, intimate, and graphic detail what I was certain they were doing. That quieted him for a while. We stayed in our position all night. First one of us slept and then the other. When morning came I told him it would be best if we confronted them. He protested weakly, but I'd have none of it. I hadn't listened to all his complaints and sat in that car all night to walk away without a conclusion.

"Here's what I want you to say," I told him. "Walk up to them when they come out to their car and say, 'I hope you had a nice evening. Did you enjoy the restaurant?'"

"I don't think I can do that, Irwin," he said pleadingly.

"It has to be done," I told him, and he finally agreed.

About an hour later, the two of them walked out to the street, arms around each other, and we approached them. My client walked up to them and said exactly what I'd told him to say. She took a long look at both of us and with great dignity said, "Good morning, Dudley." The couple then got into his car and drove away, but they knew we had them. We had established both inclination and opportunity, and I suspect we had enough to establish adultery as well, even though it wasn't necessary. His divorce was easy from that point on.

LOSING GROUNDS

I emphasize to every matrimonial client that if we are successful in establishing a case of adultery there are two ways the case can be broken: 1) If the other party catches you having sex with someone; and 2) If you go back and sleep with your spouse, and that means even if it's only one time.

In the first instance, when you have sex with a third party, you immediately place yourself on equal grounds with your spouse, that is, both you and your spouse are committing adultery and neither party has any more claim than the other.

What's interesting is that it's very common for each spouse in a divorce case to hire a private investigator to document the other's activities. Naturally, they never tell each other what they are doing, so each generally proceeds with his or her own personal affair without the slightest concern. For some reason, everyone thinks the other person is too stupid to put two and two together. Quite often the result is that each partner discovers the affair of the other, and therefore neither has a case.

And there is a humorous side to this situation. Since the world of private investigators isn't all that large, most of us know each other, if not by name, at least by sight. It's not uncommon then, that we will see and recognize each other while on a job. I can remember numerous times when I have nodded hello to one of my colleagues during a matrimonial surveillance, feeling certain that we were working on the same case—only he was working for one partner and I was working for the other.

In the second situation, if you have sexual relations with your spouse after you have knowledge of the adultery, you have, in the eyes of the law, forgiven him or her for transgressions, and that ends your chances of winning the case. Often these sexual re-unions between husband and wife are perfectly innocent and well-meant attempts to satisfy personal needs. Sometimes they are more than that.

I was working on a case where I had clearly established the fact that the wife was having an affair with another man. My client and I had confronted her with the facts, and she admitted that it was true. He then brought suit for divorce. A few days after she had been served with the papers, he got a call from her asking him to come over. She said she had something she wanted to go over with him. As it turned out, what she wanted to go over was his body. He told me: "She met me at the door in the slinkiest possible nightgown. She plied me with champagne and caviar, and before I knew it her nightgown was on the floor and we were in bed." He confided to me, "I never had sex like that with her when we were married. I don't understand it. It was great."

I said, "It's simple to understand that part of it if you think about it for a second. She's getting a whole lot of practice with the other guy." Am I a friend or what? He accepted the truth of that statement, and then I said, "More important, you just lost your case. She got you in bed and you loved it."

But it was really more than that. Her lawyer was a smart guy, and he and the wife had conspired to set my client up for the knockout. Compromised, he had no further claims for anything but a no-fault divorce. Still, judging from the smile on his face the morning after, I don't think he really cared.

That was more than ten years ago, and it seems to me the game was played a little differently then, a little more like hardball. In those days we bent the rules a bit more and we had more fun. I recently told this story to one of my coffee-drinking buddies and he agreed. "I liked it in the old days," he said. "That's when men were men, women were women, and private eyes were 'private dicks.'"

WHO IS DOING WHAT TO WHOM

Everyone is doing it to everyone else right now. Though there has been a recent drop in the number of divorces in this country, the divorce rate is still running right around 50 percent, and the amount of matrimonial work a private investigator is called on to do is enormous.

As I said, the basic heterosexual matrimonial case runs the gamut from, "I think she has a boyfriend but I still love her and can you find out for me without letting her know so we can work it out," to "I want to know just how much the bastard's got so I can get every last red cent from his grubby paws." Between these two extremes lie all the other variations on the theme.

Divorce is only one of the facets in the matrimonial diamond, however. Child custody is often an issue; premarital agreements are, more and more, part of the picture; noncustodial parents are reentering the matrimonial scene and taking custody of their children; and homosexual matrimonial matters are becoming more common.

Any and all of these issues can be part of a marriage, but if you ask, "What is the number one source of matrimonial problems?" the answer is short and sweet and you don't have to be a social worker to figure it out. It's good, old-fashioned, been with us forever S-E-X. In virtually every matrimonial case, one of the partners has sought sexual satisfaction with a third party. Remember what I just said: Beware of third parties.

Does sex explain all marital problems? Are we totally governed by our sexual needs? If I were to make a judgment based on stories I hear from my matrimonial clients, I would have to say that the answer is a resounding yes.

Now, I'm not saying that everyone has matrimonial problems, and I'm not trying to stir up trouble in anyone's bedroom, but just for your own information and enlightenment, here's a checklist one might use to determine whether or not one has a matrimonial problem based on sex:

1. *Suspicion:* Do you have the suspicion that there is something wrong or that something strange is going on with your partner? Is there something unsaid between the two of you? Experience shows that if you do have a suspicion, you will be right close to 90 percent of the time.

2. *Pattern:* Do you detect a new pattern of behavior, a new schedule at work or at home? Are things not getting done that used to get done, or are they being forgotten when they never were before? On the other hand, are things being done that were never done before (special meals, for example).

3. *Telephone:* Is the house receiving more phone calls than usual and does it seem that some of those incoming calls represent the classic case of "If a man answers, hang up?" Has there been a leap in your long-distance bill?

4. *Mileage:* Does the car need gas every time you take it out, and is the mileage mounting up faster than you think it should? When you ask about it, does your spouse say, "I haven't the slightest idea what you're talking about."

5. *Credit cards:* Are there more charges than usual, are new restaurants listed, or are there odd charges that you can't account for? These can add up to more than just dollars.

6. *New things:* Are there new clothes, pieces of jewelry, or strange matchbook covers in evidence? Is your wife sporting some sexy new underwear or is your husband using a new, musky aftershave lotion?

7. *Sexual habits:* Have they changed? Has he or she been showing off a new bag of tricks? Is he or she doing things that were absolutely out of the question for the first five years of your marriage?

8. *Telltale signs:* The scent of a perfume that isn't your own, an unexplained scratch on the back of the hand, a dreamy look in the eye, the sudden and unexplained need to go to bed early and get to the office early are all potential signs that something is amiss. Heed them.

Obviously, none of these eight items is proof of anything at all. But add any of them to number one, your basic suspicion, your gut feeling, your sixth sense that something is amiss, and you will likely find what you don't want to find.

Let me be a little more specific on each of these points and give you some hints on how to check them out:

1. *Suspicion:* After you have lived with someone for a while you get to know them. You get to know their sense of humor, their anger, their terms of endearment, their lovemaking. When any, several, or all of these things seem a bit discordant you will sense them. It might just be a little thing like a new fondness for linguini or a more obvious slip like calling you "Frank" instead of "George," but you recognize it as something slightly out of kilter. Maybe you can't even put your finger on any specifics. No matter. You sense something.

Of course, it may not be anything related directly to your marriage at all but a physical, emotional, or work-related problem that can be resolved relatively easily. Unfortunately, the chances are great that it is something related to a third party. Once your suspicion is firmly established, make mental notes of those things that seem odd or different or unusual. Don't jump to conclusions, but don't close your eyes either. For example, if Shirley goes to the store for a loaf of bread and you discover there is already a loaf of bread on the shelf, it doesn't mean that she and the baker are making dough on the side. On the other hand, if she comes home with twelve dozen sesame seed buns every two days, it's possible she at least knows the baker's first name.

I can't tell you how many cases I've had where the man or the woman starts by telling me, "I don't have any proof, but I have a feeling, something tells me that he/she is having an affair."

2. *Pattern:* One of the causes of that initial suspicion is likely to

be a change in living patterns. We all establish more or less regular patterns in our daily lives. We get up at a certain time, we exercise, we eat breakfast and go to work and so forth. When those patterns change for no apparent reason and those changes become new patterns, there is probably something more behind it than mere chance.

Here's an example. If your wife has not seen her old high school girlfriend for ten years and she suddenly starts seeing her on a regular basis, you might be a little skeptical but less than suspicious. Still, intuition (not limited to females, I might add) may be telling you to be watchful. At that point you may want to make a note of the days and times they are seeing each other. Keep tabs for a month or two. If the behavior continues, you have established a pattern of behavior that places your wife "out with her girlfriend" for four hours every Thursday night of the month. Hint: Don't always look for evening hours or even big blocks of time because people can meet before work, at lunchtime, after work, in the evenings, and on weekends.

People establish patterns that are traceable, and these can trip them up. I was once asked to try and find the source of obscene telephone calls. He placed his calls between noon and 1:00 P.M. every day. It was that pattern that led us to a man, in fact a friend of the woman involved, who made his calls on his lunch hour. It was the pattern that made me think of lunch hours and from there, with some help from the woman, we were able to find him in a phone booth and overhear his call. Patterns. Think about them.

3. *Telephone:* If you are already somewhat suspicious and you begin to note more wrong numbers or hang-ups when you answer the phone, it's time to check the phone bill. If there are new long-distance calls on the bill or the number of calls and the time spent on the phone has jumped dramatically, you should file that fact away in your mental notebook and see if the pattern continues for several months. Again, twenty-six calls to "Aunt Maude" in Idaho is not proof of anything, but . . .

4. *Mileage:* When the suspicion takes hold, you might as well follow through because you won't be satisfied until you do. When you say, "Where are you going, dear?" and he says, "I'm going to

Malone's Bar to watch the game with the boys," check it out. You know that Malone's is only three miles away, so walk him to the car and get a look at the odometer. When he gets back, ask if he had a good time, and since he's been gone six hours, ask if he stopped anywhere else. If he says "No," check the mileage. If it is substantially more than six miles, like say 119 or even 39, there may be reason to wonder.

5. *Credit cards:* As the case begins to build you will want to pay close attention to the most recent charges on your spouse's credit cards, including the gasoline cards. Note especially where the gas purchases were made. That will indicate any major changes in driving patterns. If the other credit card bills start to include items you don't recognize or items that make you wonder, like a $150 bill from a specialty lingerie shop or two tickets to a Broadway show you haven't seen, then your antennae should be up and working. (If your spouse gets his credit card bills at the office, just get the credit card numbers and call the company. Tell the representative that there is a purchase listed that is incorrect—choose one you know about for sure—and then ask the clerk to read you the rest of the purchases on that month's statement.) Also check for parking tickets. When people are having affairs they usually don't run out and stuff money into parking meters. Those tickets have a time, date, and street location on them.

6. *New things:* If there are new things around, and they just seem to appear from an unknown source, they may be coming from an unknown source. Matchbooks from restaurants where you've never eaten, movie ticket stubs, a piece of new jewelry, a pedicure, an ashtray from the Hot Sheets Motel are all indicators that something is happening.

7. *Sexual habits:* Let's face it. Sex will rear its head. When a mate is seeing someone else on a regular basis the reason is rarely intellectual. Yes, there is sex involved, and the chances are some new sexual ground is being broken by your partner. The interesting thing is, people like to show off their new talents, demonstrate their new prowess. If you detect a new sexual appetite (or one that is vastly increased or diminished), a preference for new activities or positions, or a variety of tricky moves, don't believe the line, "Why Frank, honey, I went to a porno movie with Madge and I

thought we might give some of the things they were doing a shot." It's possible but not probable.

8. *Telltale signs:* Surprisingly, when people are having affairs, they quite often leave a trail, little telltale signs that prove nothing but add to suspicion.

I have a theory that 80 percent of cheating spouses actually want to be caught. That's how the lipstick ends up on the collar and stays there. When you spot a smudge on your husband's otherwise impeccable shirt, you can be relatively sure that it's not because his secretary gave him a peck on the cheek when he gave her a letter to type.

WHAT TO DO WITH THE EVIDENCE

Let's review the situation by looking at an actual case. A young man, married less than two years, came to my office with the suspicion that his wife, Selma, was being unfaithful. Here's what transpired:

"She's acting a little strange," he told me in our first meeting.

"In what ways?" I asked.

"Well, for one thing," he said, "she started preparing these beautiful meals for me during the week and she hardly ever cooked before. Then she decided that she wanted to get to be a better bridge player. Since I don't play, she found a partner and they now play in amateur bridge tournaments out of town at least twice a month, usually on Saturday nights." Note: Saturday night is traditionally a night when regular marital partners are together, so it takes something extra special to change that pattern. Most third parties bristle because they are unable to be with their lovers on Saturday, and it is the source of much conflict in those relationships.

I definitely saw a problem there, but I said, "So far I don't see any problem."

He continued: "Maybe not, but she's also spending a lot of time talking on the phone with her partner. 'Just planning strategy,' she says. Well, she's driving to these tournaments so my car expenses have gone up, and the women all share rooms at the hotels where they stay, so that is showing up on my credit card, too. Does this bother you?"

"Not yet," I answered, lying in my teeth.

"OK, then, there's more," he said. "I've found some hotel stationery on the desk in the den from a hotel in a town where there have not been any tournaments. And finally, and this is the kicker, she has a new sexual appetite that I can't handle all by myself. She tells me it's because she's away on the weekends and she craves my body when she gets back. And now, her favorite position is standing up in a hammock. In short, Mr. Blye, I think something is amiss."

He was certainly right, only "amiss" hardly describes the problem. About a month later, he was home sick, and when the mail came he saw a large envelope addressed to his wife. He was already suspicious, so he opened it. It was the magazine of a national club that organizes mate-swapping, and there on page 39 was a picture of his wife completely nude. Underneath was her name, her measurements, and her sexual preferences—none of which he recognized from his own experience and several of which he had never even heard of.

At our next meeting he told me that in all honesty, she had tried to get him involved in swapping, group sex, and other sexual activities in the last year and he simply didn't want to do it. For weeks she pleaded with him to try it, he said, and finally he agreed to give it a shot.

"I may be a simple guy," he told me, "but I thought it was all very weird and though I might have enjoyed parts of it at the moment, it left a bad taste in my mouth."

With the magazine picture as proof, he now wanted a divorce. I agreed to handle the case, and one night I followed her and her "bridge" partner to a club where swappingly-minded couples went to meet like-minded couples. I had a female operative with me because the club did not admit singles. As we watched, our subjects made contact with two other couples and soon left; we followed them and then things took a very strange turn. All six of them went to a brownstone apartment owned by an old friend of mine. This made things a bit more complicated at first, but later, when I told my friend the story, he gave me enough information to help me support my client's case.

I could continue to give you examples of matrimonial cases, but I think by now you have the point. So let me wrap up this section with a little advice. If you decide to conduct all or part of your own matrimonial investigation, remember the first point I made—it's an emotionally draining experience. At the beginning and throughout your investigation you will ask yourself why you are doing it. Well, "why" may be the reason. People come to my office nearly every day and say, "Mr. Blye, I just want to find out why." The why of it all is a strong motivator. But while you're discovering the why you'll also be asking yourself how long it has been going on, if there have been previous affairs, and even if the other person involved is someone you know. All of these discoveries add to the emotional impact of what you're doing. Your investigation may require surveillance, tape-recording, and picture-taking of everything from bank records to the couple making love. All of these things add to the emotional impact of what you're doing.

I guess what I'm doing here is making a disclaimer, something like the warning labels on medicine bottles. In this case the warning reads: Caution—doing your own matrimonial investigation may be dangerous to your emotional health.

6

Locates, or "Where Have You Gone, Joe DiMaggio?"

"Where have you gone, Joe DiMaggio?" is a wistful phrase from a song called "Mrs. Robinson" by Simon and Garfunkel. The words symbolize a lost time, the passing of a generation, a missing feeling, but obviously not a real missing person. After all, we know exactly where Joe DiMaggio went because we regularly see him on television in his role as "Mr. Coffee." At any rate, there are, in fact, very few truly missing persons, so the legitimate missing person— Judge Crater, Amelia Earhart, Glenn Miller, Jimmy Hoffa—is much more of an aberration than the norm. People disappear, but that is a far cry from being missing, as you'll see.

In this chapter I'm going to talk about missing persons and runaways in some detail, but I'm also going to take you through the locating process so that you can do the detective work necessary to find many of the other important things that have eluded you in the past and will elude you in the future—things that run the gamut from your birth certificate to an elusive picture framer. When a private investigator talks about locates, he's not talking only about people. He's usually talking about something that falls into one of the following categories:

- Runaways
- Missing persons

- Witnesses
- Heirs
- Skip traces
- Natural parents
- Documents and property

This breakdown will give you an idea of the variety of locates I deal with, though for me, as a professional, these categories are a bit artificial and are not necessarily important. They also tend to overlap so that the distinctions between runaways and missing persons, between missing documents and other missing property are often blurred. When I'm hired for a locate, it makes no real difference to me whether I'm trying to find a person or a thing. Locating simply means locating. I go after a diamond ring with the same fervor and attention to detail that I would put into finding my cousin Louie the fishmonger who took off for the Caribbean twelve years ago and hasn't been seen since. Of course, in his case, nobody really wants to look. But before you dismiss me as a callous barbarian, a man who is capable of putting a piece of jewelry in the same category as a runaway teenager, let me say in my own defense that I prefer locating people. The reason? I'm really not a callous barbarian at all but a sensitive, kind, compassionate person with a warm spot in my heart for kids and stray dogs.

At any rate, I suspect that at one time or another, most of you have wanted to locate something in one of the categories listed above, so I will examine them one at a time, using actual cases to illustrate the points I think will be important to you.

First, however, it may be helpful to spend a minute on the definition of someone or something that is missing.

WHEN IS SOMEONE OR SOMETHING CONSIDERED MISSING?

The only really important criterion for me, and for the police, is time, and that time varies depending on the situation.

If a young child has wandered away from home and is gone for more than a few minutes the parents consider that child missing. The police, on the other hand, will advise you to wait several hours before reporting a missing child because there are many nonthreatening alternatives to those that are uppermost in a parent's mind—kidnapping and sexual molestation. Those alternatives include hiding in the house, the garage, in the backyard or on someone else's property, visiting an adult or child in the neighborhood, even talking to a harmless stranger. After all, not all strangers are kidnappers.

In a crowded environment—a shopping center, an airport, at a baseball game or a circus—the situation is more urgent when a small child is lost. But even in these cases, a few minutes of careful searching, in lieu of calling the police, will probably turn up your child. In fact, in most areas today, the police are reluctant to accept missing child reports altogether because 99.99 percent of all kids turn up in a few minutes or at the most a few hours. This isn't much solace for desperate parents, but it's a fact.

I once lost my four-year-old boy (or he lost me) at a street fair where hundreds of thousands of people were milling about. I was frantic. I found the nearest policeman and told him, arms waving, that somewhere in that giant crowd was a frightened little boy who needed his daddy. The cop calmly told me that he would turn up but that if I wanted to report him missing I should go to the precinct station. I ran the three blocks to the precinct and told the desk sergeant the story. He took my name and number, but he too assured me all would be well in less than an hour. I walked back through the entire fair calling my son's name and then gave up and went home to await the delivery of the body. When I opened the front door, my son was sitting on the floor playing happily. He gave me a big smile, and I nearly smothered him with kisses. He had gotten tired and found his own way home through the streets packed with people and cars. Maybe he was lucky but I think his case is probably typical. I was out of my mind with worry, but the child wasn't worried at all.

Young children, however, are not like teenage runaways who disappear primarily because they are having problems with their parents, so if a child has truly disappeared it is usually a police matter and the police will handle it. The child may have been kidnapped, though this is rare despite the prominence of such stories in the press. More than likely the missing child has been whisked away by a noncustodial parent involved in a custody case or by a relative for reasons unknown to the parents. I frankly have not been involved in any other type of case, and I feel that the occurrence of the other, more morbid, possibilities is rare. Teenagers, meaning in this case, young people up to twenty-one years of age, are usually considered missing within twenty-four hours. The police may not react immediately, but as a parent, I'd immediately report my teenager missing.

For adults, many police departments have a twenty-four- to seventy-two-hour waiting time before considering someone missing. But in reality, an adult is rarely considered missing because in virtually all cases that adult isn't missing—the person is not around because he or she chose not to be around. For whatever reason (and there are many) that person has decided he would rather be elsewhere.

For missing property there is really no time limit within which the item should be reported missing. Lost or misplaced credit cards should be reported immediately because they can be used immediately, but a missing bracelet may only be in another drawer or in the safety deposit box, and even if it isn't, the time limit for reporting it for insurance purposes is very generous.

But let's look at some examples to explain what I mean. The first is tragic but illustrative.

Last summer I received a call from a woman who lived on the North Shore of Long Island, an area of small, upper-middle- and upper-class communities. She told me her eighteen-year-old son had been missing from her home for four days. According to her, this had never happened before and she was very concerned. She sounded like a nice woman, and by her tone I felt she was on the edge of panic. We arranged an immediate meeting to discuss the situation.

I went to her home and during our conversation she confided to me that she had lost her entire family in Germany during the Nazi period and that she herself had been in a death camp when the war ended. When she got to this country she married an American. He was in the garment business and had done well financially in the postwar years, she said, but he had been killed in an auto accident two years before. She told me her son had been under the care of a psychiatrist for many years because he seemed unable to cope with life in general, and that he had been particularly upset since the death of his father. When we met he had been missing for nearly five days.

As I sat talking with her I noted that her face was etched with pain, not only the pain of a missing son, I felt, but the pain of her childhood, the loss of her own family in Germany, and the more recent loss of her husband. But as I said, my first rule is that I don't get emotionally involved.

As we talked we went through a list of her son's friends one by one and she told me which of them might be helpful. We went through his room, and it was clear that he had taken no clothing with him. We looked through his desk and even through his books, but we found no note. I asked if he had said anything that would give us a clue (she couldn't remember anything), and then we looked for a diary or a notebook that he might have kept hidden in a corner of the closet, in a shoebox, or under the mattress. Most parents will say immediately that their son or daughter doesn't keep a diary, but many parents think they know their children and really don't. At least they don't know them as well as they think they do. There was no cash or jewelry missing from the house. He had no car, no credit cards, no special girlfriend or male friend.

Then we talked about his habits and the things that he liked to do on a regular or semiregular basis. She told me he liked the movies, television, and reading, and that sometimes he went to a secluded spot not far from their house where he liked to sit alone under a tree and think.

I left with a list of his friend's phone numbers and the location of the tree where he liked to sit and contemplate. Since I wasn't far from that area, I decided to stop there on my way back to the office to see if there was any indication that he had been there. As I approached the tree I felt a strange sensation pass through me, a warning signal, and when I reached it, I knew why. The boy was hanging from the tree, a piece of clothesline tied around his neck, and a book at his feet. I cut him down and laid his body near the trunk of his favorite tree. I drove to a nearby gas station and called the police. Then I went back to the woman's house and told her, as gently as one can, what had happened. I gave her the book I had found lying at his feet, made sure that she called a friend, and left.

This young man was a runaway, but in his case he was a runaway from life. His case is at the extreme end of the scale, and I don't tell this story to scare parents, only to point out what running away can sometimes mean.

That same summer I had another case that was also strange and tragic but in a slightly different way. In this instance the missing person was not actually missing at all.

A woman who lived in the Philadelphia suburb of Cherry Hill, New Jersey, called me on the recommendation of a colleague of mine. She was divorced and out of contact with her husband, and when we met she explained that her daughter had run off and married a young man the mother didn't know. All of this had been done behind the woman's back, she said, and she wanted to meet with her daughter to try to mend their fences.

As we talked she told me she actually saw her daughter every few days because the girl and her young husband drove by the house. She told me her daughter would wave from the passenger seat but never called out to her. I asked if she could describe the car or tell me the license number. She could do neither. In fact, she had almost nothing more to offer except a tour of her daughter's old room, in which everything was in perfect order, as if she was expecting her daughter to return any minute. There was a closet full of clothes, the dressing table was immaculate, and there was even an open book on the night table. I asked the woman to give me the father's last known address and phone number. She did, and I left.

Again, when you've been in this business as long as I have, you get feelings about cases, and I had a strange feeling that something was wrong with what I had just heard. When I got back to my office in New York, I called the number she had given me for her ex-husband. He answered. I told him who I was and then asked, "By chance, is your daughter with you at this time?"

There was a pause and he said very softly, "No, she's with God."

"I'm afraid I don't understand," I said. "Your wife says your daughter is missing. She says she has seen her pass by in a car several times."

"I know she says that," he sighed heavily, "but our daughter has been dead for over a year. She was killed in a car accident, and my wife has never recovered from the shock. She thinks our daughter just ran away and got married."

There was no reason to doubt him. "I understand," I said. "I'm sorry for your loss. I know it must be hard to talk about it, and I appreciate the information."

"You're welcome," he said, "and I thank you for your sensitivity."

The following day I drove back to Cherry Hill and met once more with the distraught mother. I explained that I had talked with the father and I told her as gently as I could that I couldn't handle the case. She just sat there for a minute and then said, "I'm not really crazy. I just want to see my daughter again." I got up to leave and as she shook my hand she said, "I hope I haven't inconvenienced you too much."

As I was about to get in my car, I looked back at the house and the woman was standing at the window. She didn't seem to be looking at anything in particular, just staring, and I was sure that she would keep seeing her daughter regardless of what she knew or what I had said.

RUNAWAYS

The case of the runaway daughter from Buffalo, New York, will help illustrate how runaways can be found. Her father, a lawyer, was referred to me by a lawyer friend of his after his stepdaughter had been missing for several days. At first the parents thought she had run away to the bright lights of New York City, but when they didn't hear from her the next day they began to worry. As we talked, the man told me that she had certainly run away somewhere because she was the type who would do such a thing. He told me that the girl was only fifteen years old, but added, "One hates to describe one's own stepdaughter like this, but 'sexy' doesn't adequately describe her." Her real mother had not been able to control her, nor had he or his wife been able to do so. The girl smoked pot, took pills, and had several boyfriends in Buffalo and surrounding towns. I didn't ask what he meant by "boyfriends" in this instance, but I had a pretty good idea. He and his wife had found it difficult to cope with the girl as she reached her teens. "We love her dearly," he went on, "but we're nearly at the end of our rope."

I took the case—how could I refuse that plea—and the next day the couple flew down from Buffalo for a meeting in my office. As we talked I made an assessment of the parents. They were clearly well off, intelligent, and disturbed by the whole matter. Both seemed like nice people who were genuinely concerned for the girl's safety. They told me they had had discipline problems with her from the time she was ten and that they didn't like her wild life-style or many of her friends. They got specific about her friendships with boys, about her drinking habits, and about the way she behaved at home. All their concerns seemed reasonable. Then the stepfather said in conclusion, "Her actions are no longer permissible under our roof." His wife nodded in agreement.

Here are the facts as the parents gave them to me:

Name: Nancy; height 5′ 4″; weight 109; eyes blue; hair blond and cut short; no visible scars but a mole under her left arm; high cheekbones; statuesque; wears heavy, dark eye makeup and false eyelashes; last seen seventy-two hours before; wearing tight blue jeans, a white sleeveless top with red stripes, and sneakers.

Remarks: Though only fifteen she looks twenty-one and acts much older; very provocative and sexy; smokes marijuana and cigarettes; takes pills; drinks heavily; likes men of all ages.

I decided to take a look at the house where Nancy lived, and especially her room, and to talk to some of her friends, so I made reservations to accompany the couple back to Buffalo the next morning. The next day I began my investigation, and here is the procedure I followed.

I talked at great length with her parents about her eating and drinking habits (she ate mostly junk food and drank whatever was available), and whether any money or jewelry was missing from the house. Her father said that he thought she had taken about fifty dollars from his wallet but that no jewelry was missing as far as they could tell. Unfortunately she had no driver's license, no credit card, and no Social Security card, all items that are useful in tracing a runaway. (If a runaway has those documents, you can check whether driving tickets have been issued, or where bills are being run up, or whether the runaway is working.)

With her mother's help I went through Nancy's room. She had taken a minimum of clothes, but she had taken three swimming suits. I found a jar that contained the remnants of her stash of marijuana. She had not left any diary or any notes, but she had written a phone number on a piece of an envelope. (It turned out to be the number of a taxi company, but she had not used that company.) There were hard-rock records and tapes all over the room, but they didn't show a preference for any particular group. I mention this because we once located a young male runaway from Chicago by his musical tastes. He was an avid fan of the Rolling Stones, and his disappearance coincided with a Stones tour of the East Coast. On the night they were appearing at Madison Square Garden, I hired enough operatives to cover all the entrances to the Garden. They all had a picture of the young man, and even in a crowd of more than twenty thousand screaming teenagers we were able to identify him.

Next, I asked her parents to give me a rundown of Nancy's boyfriends, her other good friends, and some of those who were not so close. Often a runaway will entrust information about plans to someone who is not a close friend because he or she feels that person will be less likely to say anything. It's an interesting fact that nearly all runaways tell someone what they have in mind, which indicates to me that they want to make sure they are found sooner or later. Then I asked for a list of her favorite hangouts and an idea of the times she frequented those places.

We requested a printout of the family telephone bill so we could see if she had made any long-distance calls and so I'd be able to check her local calls as well. The phone company maintains a computer record of all local calls of two minutes or more if they are made over a sufficient distance. That distance may vary, but in general the list will not include calls within the neighborhood or even several blocks away. The distance from caller to callee has to be substantial. This listing can be requested for any purpose at all, but if it is an emergency, such as a runaway, the phone company will usually respond quickly.

I suggested to the parents that they hook up a tape recorder to the telephone immediately, so they would be able to record any incoming calls from their daughter. This is something that I advise everyone involved in a runaway or missing person situation to do because virtually all runaways and missing persons eventually call their homes.

When I mentioned the recorder, the mother said, "We've been getting some calls, two or three, in the last few days, but I thought they were wrong numbers. Nobody said anything on the other end."

"The chances are they weren't wrong numbers but hang-ups," I explained, and went on to say, "This fits a common pattern in young people. The runaway wants the comfort of hearing your voices even though she will usually not say a word." It's one of those wicked ironies of life that while the parents are usually the ones torn up by their child's disappearance and long to hear the child's voice, the "defiant" child also wants to hear the parents' voices for reassurance.

I went on: "When you get these calls, I suggest that you always talk even though she probably won't say anything. Be as nice as you can. Offer her any kind of help she needs, even offer her money. And try to find out if she is all right. Be sure not to be judgmental and not to chastise her. There will be plenty of time for that when she gets back. Keep her on the phone as long as possible. Even though you may be angry and distressed, speak calmly and say things like, 'We love you,' 'We miss you,' and 'Please let us know you're all right.'"

There are good reasons for prolonging and recording these one-way conversations. The runaway may eventually talk if you can keep the line open long enough. And if the runaway stays on the line, even silently, you may be able to tell if the call is long-distance or local. If it's local and from a pay phone the operator will ask for more money after five minutes, and if it's long-distance the operator may break in to notify the caller that the paid-for time has expired. Long-distance calls often have a light buzzing sound as well. By recording the phone call, you'll be able to replay the conversation if the runaway should talk and say things that may be important in retrospect but that you won't remember in your anxiety. You might also pick up something identifiable in the background—the sound of the ocean, an airplane, a train, a voice that gives some geographic reference, anything that might give you a clue to the runaway's location.

A third party is often helpful in negotiating with a runaway, so during these "conversations" you can also offer the services of an intermediary for the runaway to talk to. This intermediary (hopeful neutral) can be a friend of the runaway or a friend of yours that the runaway trusts, a favorite relative, or even a private investigator. I've served in this capacity many times, usually successfully.

At any rate, put the tape recorder on the phone as soon as you suspect your child has run away and keep it hooked up until the child returns.

It was midafternoon when I left their house. I had a list of Nancy's friends and her favorite hangouts in my pocket, and I decided to check out the hamburger joint where many of her friends were supposed to gather after school. The key to this case, and the key to most runaway cases, is an informant among the youngster's friends, and I wanted to start looking for that person before I returned to New York.

This friend may not come forth easily or quickly because there is a code of honor among kids that looks down on "cooperating" with adults. So, like all other people you want something from, you have to motivate them. With teens you can do this by convincing them it is for the good of the runaway, especially if the runaway is a girl. You don't have to lie because the truth is tough enough.

The truth is, many runaways end up hooked on drugs, in a prostitution or child pornography ring, or dead. Teenagers are easy prey for the vultures out there, and the cases you read about in the newspapers are only the tiniest tip of the iceberg. I have only had one tragic runaway case—the girl was found dead of a drug overdose in the basement of an abandoned building—but many run-away kids end up in the streets with people who "live" in the streets and know the laws of the street, and kids are no match for this human garbage. It's like an amateur playing with a professional; the kid doesn't have a chance. The vultures swoop down on them and offer a meal, a drink, a joint, a pill, a chance to make some fast, easy money. Then they begin the process of degrading the youngster, so that in a relatively short time the kid loses his or her self-respect. They rape both the girls and the boys, they feed them drugs and pills, and they quickly make them dependent. This street person becomes a surrogate parent responsible for feeding, providing clothes, records, whatever. The kid feels free and is probably happy, at least initially, and anything goes as long as the kid performs the duties he or she is supposed to perform. This includes prostitution (both hetero- and homosexual), performing in sex films, running and selling drugs, and degrading other kids. These youngsters are worth a lot of money on the street. Bad things DO happen so you shouldn't have much trouble motivating your potential informant if the person has any real friendship with the runaway. At any rate, you have to get the friend to work with you, and to do that you must promise that what he or she tells you will be confidential. And you have to keep that promise.

Two days later I sent a female associate of mine to Buffalo. Janice was twenty-seven at the time, but she is a good communicator and she has great rapport with teenagers. She knows how to talk and listen to them. For more than a week she hung around where she knew she would find Nancy's friends. Within twenty-four hours Janice determined that Nancy had taken a flight to California. She knew that a friend (not a taxi) had taken her to the airport. This information came partially from a friend but also because Janice knew Nancy didn't have a driver's license. A check of the records of the local taxi companies showed no trips from Nancy's address and no trips from anywhere near her home on or about the date of her disappearance. Janice also heard that Nancy had taken the flight to California on the credit card of the same friend's father. She talked with Nancy's estranged boyfriend, but he had not heard from her, probably because they had had a serious argument about a month before.

Through Nancy's other friends, Janice found out that Nancy always complained about being unhappy with her restricted life-style at home—she wasn't allowed to play her stereo after 10:00 P.M., she couldn't go out until she did her homework, and she had to do certain household chores. These may seem like sensible demands to most adults, but Nancy apparently resented them.

Janice was able to get this preliminary information because she got friendly with Nancy's friends in their own environment. This is important but not easy. Parents and adults in general are usually considered the enemies when kids are out together, and breaking that barrier is tough. You may think you're in tune with the kids, but you probably aren't. The key is to listen. In these situations you aren't there to play the parental role. If a kid should say something you disagree with completely, you shouldn't try to correct that statement even if it is dead wrong. You need something from these kids, and you may have to compromise your parental position to get it. You may even want to ask a friend of the family, preferably someone closer to the age of the young person involved, to do some of the investigating. Though it isn't a sure thing, it will probably be easier for the friend to get information than for the parents because of the built-in resistance kids seem to have to adults.

After six days of burgers, fries, and milk shakes, Janice got a tip that Nancy's destination in California had been Venice, a suburb of Los Angeles, and that she was supposedly staying with two young men in the vicinity of the boardwalk. I asked Janice if she thought the tip was legitimate and she did, so I told her to hop a plane and go to Los Angeles. Here is the rest of the story in Janice's own words.

I left Buffalo for the beaches of California, and in less than eight hours I was talking with teenage lifeguards on the beach instead of teenagers at the hamburger place. I was still eating hamburgers, however, because I had to make the rounds of the boardwalk eating spots in order to get information about Nancy.

I had her picture, but pictures have to be used sparingly. It isn't like the movies where you walk into every place in town and flash a kid's picture. People often react negatively to that kind of approach so you have to be cautious and selective. A person may be more inclined to side with the runaway than you, and if the runaway is informed that someone is looking for them, they can easily pull out and run further. So, instead of using the photo, what I did was to have two lunches and two dinners in two different places every day. This was a little hard on the waistline, but I had to start building my contacts with the people who worked in and frequented these places. I was especially interested in cultivating the waitresses because, like secretaries in an office, they know what is happening in their place and in neighboring places.

After a few days, I felt I had a sympathetic ear with one of the waitresses and I showed her Nancy's picture. She told me she had seen Nancy with a couple of guys, and she gave me the name of a third person she said knew those guys. I found the name she gave me in the phone book, called the number, and said I wanted to meet with him. We met and I explained the situation. Because I was straight with him, he gave me the address of the house where she was supposed to be.

I went directly there, parked a few doors down the street, and took up a surveillance. That afternoon, around five-thirty, two young men drove up and went in the house. I had not seen Nancy up to that point, and she was not with them in the car.

I decided to take the bull by the horns and confront the boys, so I followed them to the door and asked if I could talk with them for a few minutes. They thought I was a cop but I told them I was a private investigator and I was looking for the girl that was said to be living with them. They said she had moved out, but when I told them they had been fooling around with a fifteen-year-old minor from a prominent family, and that they would be in a whole lot of serious trouble if they didn't give me the whole story, they gave me the story.

It seems they had met her on the beach and believed her story about being twenty-two years old. One thing led to another (she had a part-time job with a photographer and wasn't earning much money), and she had moved in with them. They maintained that she had moved out about a week before and moved in with the photographer. They gave me the name of the photographer.

To make a long story short, I went to his studio, told him the story, and when Nancy came in that afternoon, I was there. I told her that her parents had sent me and that she was coming back with me. She protested that she needed to get her things, but I knew from experience that I couldn't let her out of my sight because she could easily run off again. In these cases you have to move out right away.

She was wearing only very short shorts, a halter top, and high heels, and I was afraid she'd cause a riot with that body of hers if we showed up at the airport with her dressed that way. So I took her back to my motel, gave her some blue jeans and a sweatshirt to wear, and we went to the airport.

I called Irwin to tell him I was on my way, and less than eight hours later Nancy and I landed at Kennedy Airport, where we were met by her parents and Irwin. However her parents may have felt about her escapade, they welcomed her warmly. They both thanked us and Irwin, and I walked off into the sunset.

This case took nearly three weeks to complete, and I use it to illustrate how to find a runaway because we were forced to use nearly our entire bag of investigative tricks. In summary, here is what we did:

1. Talked in detail with the parents about their daughter's interests, habits, medical and emotional problems, and the nature of her problems at home; counseled them on their role in the search; and informed them of our plans.
2. Talked with her friends and acquaintances in detail and at length.
3. Checked her room for missing items: diaries, notes, messages, maps, missing clothing, drugs, money, etc.
4. Checked phone bills for out-of-town and local calls.
5. Checked local taxi company records.
6. Attached a tape recorder to the phone.

7. Followed the initial lead to California and then as far as it took us.
8. Enlisted the help of third parties.
9. Used an identification photo.
10. Used surveillance.
11. Confronted (threatened) people with information.
12. Escorted the runaway back home.

If Nancy had used credit cards (credit card companies are cooperative in this kind of case), gotten a job with a Social Security card, contacted any of her friends or her parents (in most cases at least one friend is contacted) back home, or been picked up by local police in California or anywhere else, our job would have been considerably easier. And Nancy was more difficult to find for another reason. Unlike most runaways, she didn't really want to be found. She didn't leave any real clues, and if we hadn't gotten a reliable tip from one person she might still be missing.

I met with her parents once more after she had been returned. I said, "Your daughter could well try the same thing again in thirty days or less. That is the normal pattern."

They were surprised to hear this but assured me that things had changed and that Nancy seemed very happy at home. "That's all well and good," I said, "but let me warn you that if she does run again she will be much harder to find because now she knows how to do it right."

The role of the police in runaway cases. When small children are involved, the police, and sometimes the FBI, are called in immediately so you may be wondering why the police are not immediately involved in teenage runaway cases. There are two main reasons. The first is that parents are usually reluctant to admit to the police that their child has run away. They don't want to admit it to themselves and, if they are well known, they don't want the story to get into the newspapers or on television. In fact, in most cases the parents never notify the police, though they may quickly bring in a private investigator.

The second reason is that the police don't have the time or the manpower to handle all the runaway cases that are reported, so they tend to discourage parents by suggesting that the child will show up in a few hours or a day or two at the most. This doesn't mean they are shirking their duty, only that the dearth of police manpower is a reality. The police are more than happy to have a private investigator on the job because it takes some of the burden off them, and they are extremely helpful to PIs in runaway cases. They will provide us with all the information they can, including checks of license plates and contacts with police departments in other areas of the country.

The police have a different response to adults who are missing because adults are considered people who have left a given location and left by choice. This, therefore, is not police business. Quite often the missing person just got up and left because of any number of matrimonial, business, or health problems, or a combination of all of them. And even if they were to find the missing person, the police couldn't force that person to return as they can with an underage youngster. If this is the case, what do you do when faced with a missing adult? You will have to go it alone.

MISSING ADULTS

When an adult is missing you have some built-in help. Unlike runaways, who will gladly give up the comforts of home for their freedom, adults are less likely to give up their basic creature comforts. This will give you a pile of clues.

In the first place an adult will not normally leave on the spur of the moment. This means he or she has made plans, and often these plans include long-distance calls to friends and airplane and hotel reservations. Phone calls are a key to these preparations.

Missing adults certainly aren't going to some fleabag hotel. They are going to a predetermined place and to do that they will have made reservations. They also may get the car repaired and even purchase new luggage. An adult will usually take plenty of clothing, arrange for extra cash or travelers' checks, possibly rent a car, and certainly take credit cards. This means they almost immediately leave a trail of credit charges that can be followed like the white line down the center of the highway.

If a missing adult is going to stay with another person it won't be with someone obvious. Instead, he or she is likely to choose an old army buddy or a hometown friend he hasn't seen for years. Knowing this, you don't have to waste time going for the obvious.

When I'm called in on the case of a missing adult, I go through many of the same procedures that are listed in the summary given in Nancy's case. I'll search the home and office for notes, address books, and diaries. I'll check with the phone company, talk with the family, friends, and business associates. Not surprisingly, the office secretary is a good source of information and may well have a good lead to the missing person's whereabouts. The items in his or her desk can also be good indicators. Such things as checkbooks, airline schedules, maps, the names of travel agencies, travel guides, and so forth can provide important information. Sometimes a novel can be indicative as well. I once found a man because he left behind a copy of *Robinson Crusoe*. There were some passages underlined that indicated to me that he might be heading for a relatively uninhabited island. I checked with the travel agency in his office building and found that he had made inquiries there and had asked for information about Samoa. The travel agent had sent him to another agency that specialized in the South Seas and I discovered that our would-be adventurer had purchased a ticket to Samoa from that agency. We found our man sunning himself on the beach in a tiny village on the island. The only thing that went awry in the case was that I didn't get to locate him personally.

I've found that adults, more often than teenagers, will have confided to someone at least part of their plan, as well as the reasons for their flight from home. They may tell a friend at work, confide in a relative, or even one of their own children, while swearing the confidant to secrecy, of course. But even if the confidant only tells me something like, "He went west," that is at least a direction. With that direction, and knowing he has probably gone to a location where he has a friend, I can start making some logical deductions.

The missing person usually won't change identity or even use an assumed name at first, and this is obviously a help. And adults, unlike children, often have documented medical problems, both physical and mental. This means doctors and hospitals can be contacted in the area where you think the missing person may be headed. If the missing person takes prescription medicine, he or she will eventually need to have that prescription refilled, and pharmacies must keep records.

When it comes to telephoning home, adults are the same as teenagers. They want to be reassured by the sound of a familiar voice, so there will most likely be some hang-up phone calls. The person will generally be reaching out, essentially asking for someone to find him or her. For this reason, use the tape recorder, as mentioned above, from the very first day you determine you have a missing person situation and record all incoming calls. And remember, just keep talking to the silent line as long as it is open.

A few months ago I finished a case that involved a missing adult but also had the twist of involving a child. It was one of those increasingly common cases where an adult, a natural parent, takes a child or children with her when she disappears.

In this case, the mother took two children and left the father. Since she is a natural parent, no charges were filed and the police were not involved.

The mother in this case was an extremely religious woman, and the father was a former wrestler. He had proved his bravery in the ring for ten years, and his face bore the scars. But like so many men of proven toughness, he was gentle, soft-spoken, and polite. I say this because many women leave the home because of physical abuse from the husband. In this case there was no evidence that he had ever physically abused his wife or his children. To the contrary, he seemed especially protective of his children and concerned about the well-being of his wife. There were clearly other problems, however.

One day he came home and the three of them were gone. He had had no hint that anything was about to happen, and he had no idea where they might have gone. His wife took almost nothing for herself and very little for the children. She took very little children's clothing and that is unusual.

The father called me and we discussed the situation in detail. When we hung up I was convinced that this would be easier than most cases because of the mother's orthodox religious beliefs, which would limit the number of places she could go.

I began the investigation by going to the religious organizations in the section of Brooklyn where the family lived. I went to the schools, the houses of worship, and the social service agencies. I tried to talk with the woman's mother, but she would have nothing to do with me because she had had nothing to do with her daughter since she married out of the religion. The mother had a maid, and I talked to her at some length but unfortunately she was of little help. Maids and other service people are often good sources of information, but that wasn't true in this case. The woman's father and the neighbors flatly refused to help me.

But we did get a break when a letter arrived at the home requesting information about the family. Naturally the husband opened it and found that it had come from a small religious community in another state. He and I went there together and as we sat in the car watching the main building of the community, he recognized one of his children. It was a very emotional moment for him and when he calmed down a bit, we went to the building to talk with the director of the group.

The final disposition of this case was not terribly satisfactory for the father—the mother was allowed to keep the children—but he has been assured visiting privileges and will continue to try and reestablish his relationship with the wife and the children.

I have rarely been on a locate case where I have been unable to find the person I was looking for. I don't know if this is due to my talent, the types of situations I've been involved in, or luck. I have to think, however, that it's primarily my methods that work, and those methods have been described in these examples. You can use them in much the same way I do.

WITNESSES

Witnesses comes in two basic types: 1) those who sign documents such as marriage licenses and wills; and 2) those who see accidents or crimes. In either case witnesses are simply people who see things happen.

The document-signing witness is much easier to locate because he has done his witnessing of his own free will. Very few people have ever been physically forced to sign a document. And quite often they not only sign a name but they include an address as well. The most common problem in locating signatories to a legal document is that people readily move from place to place, and they also die. Still, a last known address can quickly lead to a live or even a dead person. All you need to do is put into practice the techniques discussed earlier in this chapter.

This is not as hard as it may sound. You don't need to hop the next jet to get what you need, because the telephone will usually be enough to get the job done. Call the post office near the last known address and see if your subject left a forwarding address. Explain the reason for your call, and you'll get the information if they have it. If you know the kind of work the person is or was in, call those types of businesses in the area and ask for help. Call the churches, the library, the schools, and the police. A clue from any of these sources will be a big step in the right direction.

Much more difficult to find, and then induce to cooperate, are the witnesses to accidents and crimes. The average guy who happens to be standing on the corner when two cars collide at an intersection may not come forth of his own free will. The driver who sees the same collision is likely to do a little rubbernecking and then ease on down the road. The drivers who are involved directly in the accident, therefore, must be alert enough to corral these potential witnesses as quickly as possible.

The best way to do this is with photographs, but after an accident you're not always equipped mentally or physically to whip out the old Nikon and squeeze off a few frames. So, you need to take note of the license numbers of the cars that are visible (write them down if you can) and try to get the names, addresses, and phone numbers of anyone around who might have seen the accident. This includes pedestrians, storekeepers, and anyone else who has a view of the street, even people on the upper floors of buildings.

I know that an auto accident, a fall, being hit on the head by a falling dumbbell, can be so disconcerting, so rattling, so traumatic, that you won't be able to perform in your normal, clear-headed manner, but the first thing you must do in these situations is focus on the task of identifying those who can help you in the future if necessary.

How do you investigate if you weren't conscious after the accident, or if you are investigating the accident of a friend or relative? Here's the way I go about it, since I'm obviously not present at the scenes of the accidents when they happen. First I go to the scene. I try to arrange to be there on the same day of the week and at about the same time of day or night the accident occurred. I observe what is going on around me, and then I begin to canvass the neighborhood. I note the license plate numbers of cars that are parked in the area and trace them to the owners, because they may have been around at the critical time. I ask people on the street if they saw the accident, and I knock on doors and ask people with windows facing the street if they saw anything at that time. I especially look for shut-ins because they are wonderful observers of the street scene. And I talk to shopkeepers who often know details of neighborhood life that customers confide in them. If necessary I will advertise in the neighborhood newspaper and even hand out flyers on the street corner, asking for information about the accident. It is rare that one of these methods fails to turn up valuable information.

HEIRS

Locating heirs is usually not much of a job. Most potential heirs are quick to show up when the time comes to divide an inheritance. If real money is involved, it's not uncommon for many of them to be on the scene immediately prior to the death of the benefactor in order to prove their fealty. That may be a little judgmental, but in my experience I've found it to be true.

Occasionally, however, there is a family oddball, a maverick who left the fold twenty years ago to join the potato rush in Idaho. Since he has been out of touch, he needs to be found so he can collect his share of the riches. He can be located by using the normal methods of drivers' license checks, last known address or addresses, or, in this case, through the Idaho Potato Association. It may take a few phone calls, but it rarely requires a field trip to find people who are not trying to hide. In more difficult cases you may have to apply the methods described in the section on locating witnesses.

If he is trying to hide you will have to employ the methods I detailed in the case of Nancy, the runaway teenager. They are considerably more involved but they may be necessary because, in many cases, the assets of an estate will not be distributed until all the heirs have been located, dead or alive.

SKIP TRACES

There are some subtle differences between a regular locate and a skip trace. A skip trace usually involves finding a person who isn't trying to hide, and in that way it is much like locating an heir. They've just moved for one reason or another. But some skips are marginal cases. They may be people who owe you money or painters who haven't finished your living room. Since the normal skip isn't consciously trying to avoid you, he is not as difficult to find. A locate is the more difficult of the two.

Take the carpenter who contracted to build a kitchen in a private house. Let's say he got a decent down payment on the job, did some of the work, and then disappeared into the woodwork as they say. He may have had a going business and just packed up and left it, or he may have been experiencing financial problems and skipped. This isn't necessarily because he does this sort of skipping for a living, though there are such cases. In essence this kind of skipper owes someone something and skips out on it, whether it's work or money or any other obligation.

How do you find a skip? First, you can assume that the person is going to continue to work and probably in the same field—a painter will paint, an accountant will account, and so forth. Also, habits will continue. A person taking vitamins will continue to do so, a person on a diet will keep eating vegetables, and a person who loves the roller derby will go to the roller derby. And most important, a person has to have a place to live. This usually means the person has filed a forwarding address with the post office or has established a post office box to receive his mail.

So, one of your first stops on this trail should be the local post office and a check of what is called the "removal book." This book is supposed to be kept for two years, and it lists all the forwarding addresses the post office has received in that period. The postal clerk may tell you the book isn't available, but remember that the book is public information and the government, with rare exceptions, destroys nothing. Your job is to motivate the clerk to dig the book out. You know how to do that from what you read in Chapter Four.

If there is no forwarding address, you can go to the last known address and begin asking many of the questions we talked about earlier. An old phone number (from an old phone book) can also yield valuable information about the current whereabouts of the person you're looking for. In doing your investigating, remember that your field is immediately narrowed because you know that your man or woman is most likely working in the same type of business he or she was in before. It's a rare leopard indeed that changes its spots. Lawyers do not become doctors and vice versa.

NATURAL PARENTS

In the last dozen years or so there has been a dramatic upsurge in the number of adopted children who have begun to search for their natural parent or parents. There has also been a counter-surge, though not as strong, of natural parents searching for children who were given up for adoption as infants.

There are any number of psychological reasons for this need to trace roots, but whatever the reasons, what it boils down to is a basic locate but a locate that presents special difficulties. The special difficulties are primarily the legal restrictions on doctors, hospitals, social workers, and adoption agencies that severely limit the release of information considered confidential.

My office handles twenty-five to thirty parent or child locates a year, and the legal restrictions notwithstanding, I have been 90 percent successful in these cases. To better illustrate the difficulties, let's look at an actual case that I brought to a successful conclusion.

I was contacted by a forty-five-year-old woman who had given up her child in the mid-1960s. She told me that she had spent more than six years in her search, had hired lawyers and private detectives before, and had been successful only in spending a lot of money—she estimated more than $25,000. The two thick folders

of documents and reports she carried were the fruits of her investment. She said she had made no progress at all.

The woman was clearly agitated, and I couldn't blame her, so
rather than putting her off by saying, "I'll read through your material and get back to you," I said, "Why don't we take the time right
now and you can tell me the facts as you know them." And I
added, "I won't charge you anything for this consultation." She
agreed. Here is what she told me.

I gave birth to a male baby in Pittsburgh on June 19, 1965.
His father, whom I've stopped hating so fiercely, had prom-
ised to marry me. Obviously, he didn't do that.

Both my parents are dead, but they were the ones who arranged for me to give up my child. They convinced me that it
was a good idea, but I'll never forget how it was done. I took a
taxi from my parents' house and had the driver stop at a specific corner in a small suburb about half an hour away. There
we picked up the couple who would be taking my baby. They
seemed nice enough, but I was only seventeen years old and
was very upset so I don't really remember a thing about them
personally or the way they looked or dressed. They gave me
five thousand dollars in cash, and I gave them the baby and
told them his name was Albert.

After we made the exchange, I had the taxi drop me off on a
side street. They kept the taxi and that was the last I saw of my
baby.

I have been living with guilt ever since that first day in the
cab. I've often wondered what happened to my boy, what he
looks like, if he's smart, and if he's happy. It's very hard living
with all that accumulated baggage, and that's why I started
looking for him about ten years ago. I wanted to find him and
make sure he's all right and I wanted to see what he looked
like. I don't want a big scene, and I don't want him to come
back to me. Just to see him is really all I want.

That's essentially it. The lawyers and the private detectives
I've hired in the last few years have come up with this stack of
paper, but there really isn't anything here that will help you,
as far as I can tell. I don't actually have a clue to where my
boy is or whether he's alive or dead.

When she stopped I asked a couple of questions, the first of which was, "What was the baby's full name at birth?"

"Albert Lukas," she said. "Lukas was my family name."

Then I asked, "Do you recall the last name of the people who adopted the child?"

"Yes, it was Baker," she answered. "I'm afraid it's fairly common."

"I'll find him," I said confidently because I knew I'd be able to do the job in one or two days at the most.

She looked at me cautiously and then said, "What will it cost me, Mr. Blye?"

"About a hundred and fifty dollars," I said. "Certainly no more than that."

"That's all?" she asked, as though there was something wrong with me. I could understand her question. After spending more than twenty grand to find nothing, how could she expect to get anything for a measly $150?

"That's all it will cost," I said.

Two days later I found the young man, and I called her and told her where to find him. She was incredulous. "You mean that after all these years of looking you found him in two days?"

"Yes," I said, "and I knew I'd find him while you were sitting there the other day telling me the story. It might have taken a day or two more, but I was absolutely certain that I'd be able to locate him."

We met in my office the next morning. She was ecstatic. She reached in her purse and pulled out a check for $500. "That's three hundred and fifty too much," I said.

"No, it isn't," she replied. "You did a magnificent job and you deserve the extra money. But tell me, how did you do it?"

She deserved to know, so I told her how it was done.

When you first started looking for your child he was only about eight years old. That's one of the reasons it was so hard for the lawyers and detectives to find him. You stopped looking about six years later when he was about fourteen.

Let me ask you a rhetorical question. What is the first thing a boy does when he reaches the age of sixteen or eighteen? The answer is, he get a driver's license. Kids can't wait for the big day. I myself couldn't sleep for weeks waiting for my eighteenth birthday. All I could think was "I'm going to drive." Things haven't changed.

At any rate we knew his date of birth, his first name as a baby, your last name, and the last name of the adoptive parents. I called a friend at the state department of motor vehicles, gave him the date of birth, and asked him to do a computer search on the name Albert with the last names of Lukas and Baker. (Normally, forms have to be submitted to get this information; the forms are available from the department of motor vehicles in every state.) We found him under Albert Baker, and the address is on Long Island. It was actually very simple.

She was too pleased to be amazed at my skill and speed, but that's how it was done. She was one happy lady when she left my office, and I felt good for her.

I knew how to make this search and anyone could have done the same thing, though it might have taken an amateur a bit longer. I figured the boy was probably still somewhere in the New York area, but if he had been elsewhere, I could have run the same check in every state. True, he could have changed his first name, but that isn't the way people normally do things. The adoptive parents got a baby that was already named so they were likely to keep that name.

Here are some other things I could have checked if it had been necessary. The first is the cab ride during which the woman exchanged her baby with the other couple. Even though that ride took place twenty years earlier, it is possible that the trip could have been traced through company records (if the company still existed) and that the driver might be found. This is not an everyday experience and the driver, if alive, is probably still telling the story to his friends at the local tavern every chance he gets.

I could also have checked draft and voter registration records under the combination of names I had, and the enrollment records of the various colleges in the area. If none of these checks had turned up anything, then the case would have become more difficult. You'll see just how difficult in the next example.

The case above, that of a natural parent wanting to find his or her child, is a bit unusual. The reverse is more often the case. That is, I'm asked by the young adult or a person in his early thirties who was adopted at birth to help him find his natural mother and father. This is a tougher proposition, but it can be made considerably easier if the adoptive parents are willing to cooperate in the search. I've found that most parents will help because they want their child to get through this period in his or her life as smoothly and with as little trauma as possible.

I'd estimate that about 80 percent of all adoptive parents know something about the natural mother. If this includes a last name and last known address, so much the better. If they only know the city the mother was from it is a good start.

With close questioning, the adoptive parents may remember the name of the hospital, which makes searching birth records easier, especially if the child's last name is a common one. The hospital itself may not provide much information, but you can check birth records at the local health department if you have a name and a date of birth. An address is also helpful. It isn't a complicated process. Adoption agencies are not good sources either, but they can often be convinced to pass along your letter of inquiry to the natural mother. Be prepared to ask them to do this if all else leads to a dead end.

But if you have that last name and it isn't too common, you can take the next step. Using an old *Cole's Directory* (a reference guide available in most libraries that lists addresses, names, and phone numbers; see Chapter Eleven for more information on *Cole's*), you can trace that name to an address. You can then use *Cole's* to reverse the process and that address will help you find the names of people who lived in the same block or same neighborhood at the time of the child's birth. Then you have to take a current phone book and look up those neighbors' names a second time. Some of them may still live in the same area and if they do, you're in luck.

But now the real legwork begins. You can either call the people you have found in the phone book or go back to the neighborhood and start knocking on doors. You may find a neighbor who remembers something about the family, about the mother, or about the situation. You may even find the parents themselves, though that is rare. But there would have been gossip about an unwed mother in those days, and any piece of information can help. Local merchants and the neighborhood school can also be of help. Then you can talk with the local ministers and ask them to check church records for the family name or a baptism. What you desperately need in this kind of case is someone who remembers the family, the girl, or the situation. Once you find that person you have a decent chance of tracing the parents.

Today, many previously confidential records are available from the federal government under the Freedom of Information Act, and this act and the information that it provides access to can be a valuable tool in the hands of the investigator in this type of case and in many others. What the FIA does in this type of situation is allow you to check the records of government agencies that might have assisted the mother's family or the mother herself. If the family was on state welfare or received federal aid of any kind, you may be able to trace it. The problem here is time and obstructionism. You're likely to get a firm no at every door, but if you do, then you should ask the agency how to go about getting the information. "I need your help" is a powerful phrase. So are "I'm confused" and "How would you do it?" Remember that bureaucracies use "There's no way" as part of the first line of defense. You have to be ready to say, "Well, now that we have that out of the way, tell me what I need to do."

DOCUMENTS AND PROPERTY

Of all the things that people want to locate, documents and personal property are the easiest. Still, I have hundreds of requests each year from people who have misplaced this piece of paper and lost track of that painting and want to find it. Much of it isn't worth finding as far as I'm concerned, but what some people regard as junk not worth looking for, other people regard as extremely valuable property worth time and money to find. A dress, a piece of jewelry, an antique vase, a pet, or a book can be lost treasure to the person who wants to find it. Documents like deeds to property, birth or marriage certificates (the availability of these varies from state to state), certificates of adoption, leases, and court records in some states are all available and they require the basic investigative work discussed earlier.

Here's a simple example of what I mean. A few years back a woman came to my office and asked me to help her locate the man who had framed some of her paintings several years before. The frames had been handmade and she liked them very much. She now had some new paintings that she wanted framed in the same way with the same wood, and she wanted to use the same picture framer.

The problem was, the picture framer was not in his old location when she drove by to see him, and the telephone directory no longer had a listing. She reasoned he had either died (and she said that was unlikely because he had been a relatively young man) or had moved to another area. She had looked for ads in the newspaper but found none.

The most likely explanation was that he had simply moved to another city and maybe another state. The latter seemed the most likely case. But where? I did the simplest thing of all. I went to my directory of organizations and associations and found one that had some relation to picture framing. I called the association, asked them to check their records, and they found the man I was looking for in Louisiana.

It's easy when you know how to go about it, and now you know how to go about it.

7

Surveillance: On a Clear Day You Can See Hoboken

Here's how a surveillance is depicted on television.

An unmarked police car is parked at the curb for two minutes. A subject comes out of a building, gets in a car, and pulls away. The cops pull out immediately and follow him. They follow closely for one minute. The subject suddenly realizes that he is being tailed and speeds up. The cops follow suit. A terrific high-speed chase ensues. Pedestrians scatter in all directions. The two cars fly through intersections, leaving half a dozen battered cars in their wake. There are nine near collisions and then the subject loses control of his car and plows into a light pole. The cops jump out and collar the guy. End of scene. (Elapsed time four minutes.)

It's all extremely dramatic and exciting, and pure fiction. And yes, I know that action must be condensed for television. Still, here are just a few of the things that are inaccurate in this scene:

• A surveillance always takes a lot of time; subjects don't show up a few minutes after you take up your position; a few hours is more like it, and it can be days.
• You should never follow your subject the instant he starts to

move, whether in a car or on foot; there needs to be a little distance between the two of you.

• People don't normally notice they are being followed unless
you do something strange to attract their attention; sometimes
even honking your horn won't alert them.

• High-speed chases happen so rarely that they make headlines
when they do occur. Usually, if the person being followed starts to
speed up, the following car doesn't speed up, it just lets the subject
go.

Other than these few small points, the action is right on the
mark—at least when I'm speaking with tongue in cheek. To put
things into perspective, here's an example of what happens on a
real surveillance.

> After slumping in the passenger seat of my car for two and a
> half hours, I see my subject leave his office. It's 8:45 P.M. on
> an early summer evening. He gets into a blue four-door Buick
> and pulls out of the parking lot. I wait until he gets to the
> street and then begin to follow him, not yet turning on my
> lights. Only when I pull into the traffic do I switch my lights
> on low, never on bright.
>
> I follow him, trying to allow at least one car to come be-
> tween us at all times. When we come to a traffic light, I pull to
> his right and try to position myself in that blind spot that ex-
> ists in the right rear (at about five o'clock to the driver), in
> most cars, an area that the driver can't see. I continue to fol-
> low him and in about ten minutes he pulls up in front of a
> tavern, parks in a small lot, and goes inside. Again I wait.
>
> At 11:05 he comes out, and we start the process all over
> again. I let him get started, then I follow at a discreet distance,
> and he doesn't have the slightest idea he is being followed. As
> he pulls into his block, I hang back at the corner, then I turn
> my lights off and follow him to his house. He parks in the
> garage and goes into the house. It is 11:40 P.M. (Elapsed time
> almost three hours.)

Of course, I did some homework before I took up this surveillance and some more work when I got to the parking lot outside

his office building. I knew who the subject was, and I knew his car. I also knew where he lived, so when he left work I had a pretty good idea of where he was ultimately headed. What I wanted to find out was where he went before he got home. To establish the fact that I was in that parking lot at that time, I made a note of the makes and models of the cars parked near me in the lot in front of his office building, and I wrote down their license plate numbers.

Then, before he came out I did something that is extremely important. I took a mental picture of the shape of the back of his car with special attention paid to the shape and size of the taillights. I also noted that he had a bumper sticker on the right rear bumper, an automobile club sticker on the left side, and a tail pipe that was bent down and to the right. With that mind-picture of the rear of his car I would be able to pick up his image, especially his taillights, even if we got separated.

Before I tell in detail how to conduct a surveillance, both on foot and in a car, I want you to take a good look at the following basic guidelines.

1. *Verify your subject.* Make absolutely certain that you have the right person or the right car, van, motorcycle, whatever. Remember the story I told earlier about following the wrong man for an entire weekend because he had been misidentified. That one still gives me nightmares.

2. *Don't worry about losing your subject.* It is infinitely better to lose someone than to "burn" the surveillance because he suddenly realizes he is being followed. "Burning" means that you've been spotted. If you do get burned, the job is over, at least for you. Someone else can take over another day, but it's the end for you. If you lose the subject, you can always pick him up again. Tomorrow is another day. This is something many professionals never seem to learn.

3. *Blend in with your surroundings.* If you're following by car, don't drive a red Corvette with the top down. If you're on foot, wear grays and beiges. Wear shorts in Miami and slacks in New York. Don't be conspicuous. This means leaving your Groucho Marx disguise at home.

4. *Make yourself as comfortable as possible and keep eating and drinking to an absolute minimum.* There is no quicker way to blow a surveillance than to have to go to the bathroom at a critical moment. The problem is, of course, that you never know when that critical moment may occur.

5. *Be prepared.* Have everything you think you could possibly need with you. If you have to make a quick phone call and you don't have any change you're in trouble. If you drive up to the toll booth with a twenty-dollar bill, you will lose valuable time and possibly your subject. In an area where you might have to use public transportation, be sure to carry the correct change or a token. There is nothing like waiting in line at the token booth and watching a subway train with your subject on it pull out.

6. *Have the right equipment.* Double-check everything before you head out to the street. There will be no time to stop for batteries for your tape recorder, film for your camera, or other supplies.

7. *Be patient and vigilant.* You know how all you have to do to make the phone ring is to leave the room? Well, all you have to do to miss your subject is to give up too easily, or sometimes even to turn your head for a minute. It's going to be difficult but you will have to maintain your surveillance even when you are so bored the top of your head is about to come off. Someone once said that patience is a virtue. On a surveillance (and in most of the other work a PI does) patience is the first commandment.

I'm aware that the professional private investigator has a distinct advantage over the amateur in at least one respect. The people I am hired to keep under surveillance are not known to me, and I am not known to them. There is a strong possibility, however, that you will be known by the people you put under surveillance. Your spouse, your children, your friends, your business associates will all recognize you easily if you aren't extremely careful. This places an added burden on you, and it may temper the way in which you conduct your surveillance and the decision of whether or not to do it yourself.

One way to make yourself less conspicuous is to rent or borrow a car to do your surveillance. Just make sure you get a car that won't draw special attention. And don't forget those sunglasses.

But sunglasses or plain car notwithstanding, you may be spotted. Still, except in obviously awkward or peculiar circumstances, you can probably pretend that your meeting is accidental—after all, you have as much right to the road or the shopping center or the sidewalk as the person you're following. Still, it's always a good idea to have an excuse ready. "I'm meeting so-and-so here and we're going to do such-and-such" is usually good enough. You can be on the safe side, however, by contacting a friend beforehand so he or she can corroborate your story if need be. But don't expect to be ignored. The person you're following is more likely to challenge your presence than ignore it because even though he may be guilty of some indiscretion, survival instincts take over and he will try to put you on the defensive.

Now let's take a closer look at the seven guidelines I just outlined above.

VERIFICATION

The verification of the subject is incredibly important. If you are conducting a surveillance on someone you know, verification is not an issue. But suppose you don't know the person well, you don't know his car, his street, or his neighborhood. Suppose you only have a picture of your wife's boyfriend, your husband's girlfriend, your daughter's fiancé, or your partner's wife. This puts you in a different ball game—the same one I'm in.

I use the following rule of thumb. If I'm at all uncertain about having the right person, I don't pick up the surveillance. You can save a lot of time and energy by waiting until you're sure. And never try to verify your subject by confronting him or her directly with the old "Got a match, buddy?" ploy because people are quick to recognize a ruse. It takes very little to put someone on the defensive and a person on the defensive is suspicious and difficult to follow.

LOSING YOUR SUBJECT

When I'm following someone, I have a rule that is immutable, unchangeable, absolutely written in stone: It is better to lose the subject than for him to recognize you. This is a bugaboo for most amateurs. A feeling of panic sets in when it appears that you are about to lose your prey. I urge you to try and be philosophical about it. If you lose him, you're just like the rest of us because we all lose them.

I've been burned on occasion, but it hasn't happened to me often. That's because I'm careful.

I got this way through practice, so I suggest that you practice both foot and car surveillances on total strangers. While you're driving to work one morning, pick out a car and follow it. Try to stay out of the driver's mirrors. Hang back a good distance and see if you can still keep him in sight. After you're satisfied that you have the hang of it, do the same thing at night and don't forget the importance of the rear profile of that car. On the other hand, don't be like the guy I was training one day who insisted on following our subject's car so closely I felt we were attached to the guy's bumper like a trailer. My man was so intent on staying close that when our subject pulled into a New Jersey Turnpike toll plaza to pay the toll my trainee actually bumped into the back of the subject's car. Surprisingly, it didn't turn out as bad as it sounds because after that, there was no way our subject could think we were tailing him: Tails don't bump into their subjects. Still, it's important to maintain your distance.

You carry on foot surveillance in much the same way, and you can also practice it in the same way. Pick a crowded street and follow a randomly selected subject for several blocks. After you have an idea of what it's like, move to a less crowded street and try the same thing.

Then follow someone into a store and you'll get an idea of how difficult tailing someone can really be. After all, what do you do with yourself while the subject spends ten minutes looking at a tie? One thing you can do is look at ties too, but you're better off if you go to another counter where you can still see your subject and busy yourself with the after-shave lotion. Let me tell you one thing not to do. Don't lean against a pillar reading a newspaper. We don't do that anymore.

And don't worry. You aren't committing a crime by following a person. Besides, in a random practice surveillance, you're the only one who knows what's going on, and it's more of a game than anything else.

BLEND IN

Blending into your surroundings is one of the keys to good surveil-lance. One of my operatives is an attractive young woman, the kind of person you would normally notice in a crowd, but she is a master when it comes to blending in wherever she is working. I've passed her in the office thinking she was a client, and then done a double take when I realized it was Virginia. It isn't because she wears disguises, she just has the ability to look as if she belongs—whether it's at the opera, the ball game, or in the corner deli. And please note—blending in is the opposite of wearing a disguise. For the most part people are uncomfortable in disguises; that discom-fort becomes obvious to the subject you're following.

Dress for the occasion. If you're on the street, wear street clothes and make sure they're in neutral colors. Bright colors like red and orange attract the eye, and it only takes a glance from the corner of your subject's eye to cause problems. Stick to beiges, browns, and muted shades. If you're on the beach, wear a bathing suit and make it neutral, too. I don't care if you have the body of a Greek god, wear a normal bathing suit instead of a low-cut piece of cloth that barely covers your loins. This goes for women too. Strikingly tiny bikinis attract every eye on the beach. I use the beach only as an illustration, since you are not likely to work the beach very often; the same rules apply everywhere.

If you're sitting in your car at night, don't smoke. The light from a cigarette is like a beacon, especially in the suburbs. When you're parked, never sit in the driver's seat. Use the passenger seat so people will think you're just waiting for the driver. If there is an-other person with you, have that person sit in the left rear seat.

PERSONAL COMFORT

There is no way to convey to you the sheer boredom and physical discomfort of maintaining a long surveillance. Normally you have to keep your eyes on one place—a doorway, a window, a house, a street corner—for several hours without wavering. It takes only an instant for your subject to appear at that spot and another second for him or her to disappear. If you let your attention flag and the subject shows up, that's the end of it, at least for that particular time. You can't read, you can't do crossword puzzles, you can't watch a portable television set. Total concentration is what matters; it is everything. The only safe thing to do to pass the time is listen to the radio or talk with your partner if you have one.

But I should warn you that on a long surveillance, not only does time creep like a slug, but your partner can easily become a harpy. After a few hours friends can become mortal enemies. In other words, silence is often golden. If there was a way to reduce the tedium, I'd be glad to tell you about it, but I've been at it for a long time and I have yet to find a way of decreasing the boredom of a surveillance.

I have, however, developed some guidelines for my physical comfort, and they apply to what I wear and what I eat.

First and foremost, I eat very little and drink less. I'm especially careful of how much coffee, tea, or hot chocolate I drink, and any drink with caffeine should be taken in moderation. Since you are not going to be near a bathroom of any kind you want to minimize the stress on your kidneys, stomach, and bowels. Liquid does just the opposite, and in a big hurry. Therefore, follow this hard and fast rule. Don't drink coffee before you go to the job. If you must drink coffee while you're there, immediately pour half of it out of the container as soon as you buy it. This may not be too satisfying or economical, but it will keep you from drinking the whole container. Don't bloat yourself with liquid—and kidney-stimulating liquid at that.

Be careful of food intake prior to and on the job. It's all right to eat on the job (and necessary to keep you alert) but do it moderately and be careful in your choices. Don't eat anything with oil, mayonnaise, or salad dressing. This includes cole slaw, potato salad, egg salad, tuna salad, or any other prepared salads because they contain oil and mayonnaise and these elements agitate the stomach. Stick with processed cheese, turkey, or ham and stay away from the processed meats like turkey roll and olive loaf. If there are certain foods that tend to upset your stomach you obviously need to stay away from them.

When dressing for your surveillance you should make yourself as comfortable as possible while paying close attention to the weather. Overdressing is better than underdressing because you can always peel off a layer of clothes. It's hard to run out and buy a sweater if the weather suddenly turns cold.

Regardless of the cold, however, don't wear wool since it can get scratchy after a while. Don't wear blue jeans because they're too tight-fitting. Cotton is all right but not great because it stains easily. What does that leave? Those good old man-made fibers. And of these polyester is best. You can just toss it in the washer and twelve hours of food stains and sweat wash right out. It's one less thing to worry about. I usually wear chinos in a tan shade, and for this purpose I have at least a dozen pairs that are almost identical. I call them my surveillance pants (some people have safari clothes, don't they?) because they are totally nondescript. To the chinos I usually add a lightweight sweatshirt. A pair of sneakers completes my ensemble. I'm not going to win any awards for this outfit, but it is comfortable, and comfort is the key.

Of course, if I am on a case where I know that I will be seen in a restaurant, a theater, or at a social function, I dress accordingly. For these times I have a collection of dark blue and gray suits (some with thin pinstripes) and unobtrusive striped ties. I try to look like a cross between a banker, a lawyer, and an accountant, so that I can blend in with any crowd.

BE PREPARED

Boy Scouts are always prepared and you will have to be, too. Carry plenty of change for the telephone and for highway and bridge tolls. Nothing will hang you up like having to search for toll money while your subject is going from zero to sixty in 8.4 seconds. Plan it so that you not only have the right change but that you have it close at hand, that is, in some kind of container that is not in your pocket. You don't want to be delayed for any reason. Also carry enough cash for normal expenses and a credit card or two in case you have abnormal expenses. A checkbook is a good thing to have on hand as well.

Carry a three-by-five-inch index card with a list of all the phone numbers you may need to call. Let at least one person know where you are, and where you are likely to be, and try to arrange it so that person will be available to serve as a contact or relay if you need any kind of assistance.

If you have any reason to believe that you might need something, take it with you. The worst that can happen is that you end up not needing it. This includes things like aspirin, prescription medicine, cough drops, breath mints, Band-Aids, Kleenex, and so on. You may look a little bulky if you carry all this stuff, but you won't have to worry about needing something you don't have.

EQUIPMENT

Here is a checklist of equipment you will need on an ordinary car surveillance (also see Chapter Twelve).

1. *Wide-mouth plastic bottle.* This may be a somewhat delicate subject, but when you need to go you need to go, and the "jug" has saved me on many a job. Men clearly have an advantage in this area. If you're a woman you have a bit of a problem. One of my female operatives got so tired of having to search for indoor bathrooms that she got in the habit of wearing a skirt without panties. In that way she could use the jug almost as easily as a man. I don't honestly recommend this for women, but to each her own.

2. *Tape recorder.* Buy an inexpensive tape recorder for noting locations, physical details of buildings, license plate numbers, routes of travel, fragments of conversations, and anything else that you think may be pertinent in a case. Be sure to bring plenty of tape and extra batteries.

3. *Note pad.* You will want to have a pad—I use a pocket-size spiral notebook—to make notes for quick reference. You may want to note such things as physical descriptions of subjects and driving directions without whipping out your tape recorder. Don't forget several ballpoint pens.

4. *Camera.* An inexpensive camera with a decent lens is a must. Photos are icing on the cake of evidence. Take as many as you think will be useful in documenting your case. This means you

need to carry a supply of film, and batteries for the camera if it needs batteries.

I prefer one of the auto-focus models with an SLR lens because you don't have to waste time focusing and the good ones indicate by voice or beep if there is sufficient light for a picture. They also advance the film automatically so they have the additional advantage of one-hand use. This means you can even take a picture while driving.

If you have a fancier camera with a zoom lens you may want to take it along with you if your surveillance is being done from a car, but if you're not careful that kind of camera is more likely to result in a blurred picture of a tree than in a picture of your subject.

5. *Sunglasses.* This may seem like a rather frivolous piece of equipment, but it isn't. First, sunglasses serve to partially hide your face, which is good for surveillance purposes, and second, they protect you from being temporarily blinded by the sun. One of my best investigators came into my office late one summer afternoon with his tail between his legs.

"I lost the guy," he said. "The sun got in my eyes and by the time I was able to focus again, he was gone."

I commiserated. "It happens," I said, but since I'm also the boss, I added, "How could an experienced guy like you let that happen?"

"I don't know, Irwin," he said, "but it just didn't enter my mind to put on sunglasses. It won't happen again."

Enough said.

6. *Binoculars.* In many cases a small pair of binoculars will come in handy. You never know when you'll need to get a close-up of your subject or anything else. I was on a case one day when I noticed some strange activity down the block from where I was sitting. I couldn't make out what it was so I took out my binocs for a closer look. What I saw was two guys breaking into the trunk of a car. I hopped out of my own car and ran to the opposite corner, where I dialed 911 and reported a robbery in progress. In less than a minute there was a squad car at each end of the block, and they caught the two guys red-handed. That may not have anything to do with your immediate needs, but it shows you how useful this piece of equipment can be.

7. *Maps.* A street map and a highway map are good things to keep in the glove compartment. You may have to drive to a strange area of town or hit the road out of town without notice. It's always good to know where you're headed and how to get back.

PATIENCE

I can't teach you patience because I have enough trouble sitting still myself, but I can give you one piece of advice. Your subject is the director of the show when you're on a surveillance. When he or she moves, you move. When he or she doesn't move, you don't move. It's sort of like a board game, only you never get to throw the dice.

Accept the fact that you can only do your job by staying on the job.

Now let's look in even more detail at some of the critical aspects of surveillance, and I'll pass along some professional hints that I think you'll find useful and even fascinating.

SURVEILLANCE BY CAR

The best way to explain how to conduct an auto surveillance is to describe an actual case for a client who was certain his wife was having an affair with a younger man who worked in his restaurant. My client told me that Sunday morning was the time he thought the two were meeting, so we made plans for me to begin my surveillance the following Sunday.

That morning I parked about half a block from the apartment building where my client and his wife lived. Though she normally did not leave for her alleged rendezvous before eleven, I got into position at nine, just to be on the safe side. I'm never late. In fact, I'd rather be an hour early for anything than five minutes late.

My client's apartment had a balcony that overlooked the street and when his wife left the apartment he was going to come out on the balcony and give me a hand signal.

I had been given a picture and a description of his wife, but I had never seen her in person. From her picture she appeared to be attractive, slim, and about forty years old. I also had her license plate number and had looked closely at her car, a gray Cadillac, in order to get its shape and size clearly in my mind. At about ten-thirty two women came out of the building and went in different directions. Neither looked exactly like the picture or the description I had, but one of them was a definite possibility. I looked up at the balcony and sure enough, there was my client, in his bathrobe, signaling madly and pointing in the direction of the woman who I had thought might be his wife. Unfortunately, she was already getting into a car (his car, as I later found out) that was parked heading in the opposite direction. My client was waving his arms and generally making such a commotion that the neighbors were coming out to see what was going on. His wife, probably intent on getting started, didn't notice what was happening, but I had to figure out a way to get pointed in the other direction.

As she was starting the motor in his car, I pulled away and drove as quickly as I could without looking like a hot-rodder to the other end of the block, where I made what I thought was an inconspicuous U-turn. Then I waited in my lane for her to get started. It took a minute or so for her to maneuver out of the parking space and by that time there was a car behind me honking to get by, which wasn't so bad except that a honking horn tends to attract attention. But I held my place and she finally pulled out and I started slowly up the block.

I didn't want to get too close, so I was creeping forward and the guy behind me was blasting away with his horn. I was getting mad, but one of the things you can't do is get into any kind of altercation with another driver because that not only calls undue attention to you but ends up causing you to lose your subject. I thought to myself, ''This whole thing is not starting out in an auspicious manner.''

Finally, she turned left at the corner and I was able to speed up, wanting desperately to give the guy behind me the finger. Let me point out here that if it had been dark I would not have turned on my lights immediately after leaving the curb, but once my lights were on I could have moved up behind her more quickly because she wouldn't have been able to see into my car. (If it had been dark I also would have given the guy the finger.)

I continued to follow her, always letting one car get between us.

We'd only gone about a mile when she pulled up to a bus stop and opened the passenger door. A young man who had seemingly been waiting for a bus got in beside her. She drove in a random pattern—a right turn, straight for two blocks, a left turn, straight for three blocks and so forth—for a few minutes and headed for the expressway. All this time I had stayed nearly a block behind her and had no trouble whatever keeping her in sight.

When we got onto the expressway I moved into the center lane and let her get two blocks ahead. I knew that all the exits were on the right side so by staying in the center I'd be able to move into either of the other two lanes without difficulty. Thanks to her husband, I had an idea of where she was going. (You may find following a car much easier with a partner. With two people, the driver can concentrate on traffic and not the subject car. The partner doesn't pay any attention to the traffic but keeps his eyes on the subject car, giving the driver information like, "It's the second car on the right, now the third, just pulled into center lane directly in front of the car in front of us." This running commentary is extremely useful in heavy traffic.) When I could see the correct exit sign, I moved into the right lane, since I was fairly certain she would be doing the same and should be unable to see me because of the natural blind spot that exists in most cars. Besides, her male friend had moved over next to her and she was obviously too involved to take notice of anything but the road ahead and probably not much of that.

As her friend began nibbling at her ear I was reminded of another time when my old partner and I were tailing an older woman and her young boyfriend, who was driving. We had her husband, who happened to be an old friend of ours, with us. He was in the backseat and most of the time we had him keep his head down so his wife couldn't spot him. From time to time he'd ask us what they were doing. My partner looked at me and we started a routine. The couple was actually doing nothing, just sitting side by side, but I said, "Freddie, you don't really want to know."

"Yes, I do," he answered. "Please tell me."

I winked at my partner and said, "Harry, what do you think they're doing?"

"I think she's kissing him on the neck," Harry said. There was a little groan from the backseat.

"What's she doing now, Irwin?" Harry asked me.

"Look's to me like she's sucking on his ear lobe," I answered. There was more groaning.

"Uh, oh," Harry said. "Where'd her head go?"

"I don't know," I said. "I can't see it but the car is all over the road."

"OK, you guys, that's enough," Freddie said, from the back. "If either of you says another word, I'll break your heads."

"It was all in fun, Freddie," I told him. "They really aren't doing anything at all."

"Very funny, you sadists," he said.

That might have been a bit unkind of me and Harry, but a little kidding between friends is in order from time to time. Besides, we told him we were kidding.

Back to the road, however. I continued following the two lovers until they pulled into a motel about forty miles north of the city. There was a gas station across the street and I pulled in there. I pumped some gas while I watched them check in. They then drove into the motel lot and parked in front of a room, but from that distance I couldn't make out the number. I watched as they went in, then I paid for my gas and drove across the highway to the motel.

I parked about three doors down from theirs. I got out and took several pictures of her car, and the motel room in the background, noted the license plate numbers on two other cars in the motel lot, and then walked over to the office. I asked the man behind the counter for a room.

I registered and then said, "I'm a private investigator and it would be very helpful to me if you would answer a couple of questions about the couple that just registered. Have they been here before?"

He looked at me a little funny and then said, "Yeah, they come here about every week," and with that he took out the registration card. It was signed with a phony name but that didn't matter because, if necessary, a handwriting expert would be able to identify it. Not all clerks are so helpful, but I find that if you don't apply any pressure they will usually respond. In this case the guy even made a photocopy of the card for me.

"Thanks very much for the help," I said, and as I shook hands with him I gave him the twenty-dollar bill that was in my palm. He just smiled.

When I can, I take a female operative with me on a case like this and we walk into the motel office right behind the couple we're tailing. As we stand there arm in arm waiting our turn I make sure I get a good look at the registration card number and the name that the couple is using. After that I can always call the motel and ask them to check their records on that date by the card number and name. But if I judge the clerk to be a potentially helpful person, I may just go ahead and do all of that as I register.

I went back to my car, moved it even farther away from their room, and sat down to wait. About an hour and a half later, they came out and I took a picture of them arm in arm. They drove away and I didn't need to follow because I actually had all the information necessary to make a case. Besides, I wanted to do a bit more at the motel.

The maid comes to clean up quickly in these "hot sheet" places (the term given to motels and hotels that cater to three-hour guests) and when she got there a few minutes later I told her I'd like to look around the room before she cleaned up. I gave her five dollars to make it worth her while to wait.

I wanted to check out the room to see if there was anything there that would be helpful to my client's case. What I found turned out to be useful. There was a paper cup with lipstick on it, an empty wine bottle, the receipt for the room, a matchbook from the restaurant owned by the woman's husband, the foil wrapper from a condom, and an empty package of Marlboro cigarettes. All of these items, except the condom, could be traced back to my client's wife. The lipstick on the cup was her shade, the matchbook and wine came directly from the restaurant and she was known to like that vintage, and the cigarettes were her brand.

In one afternoon, I had established a complete case for my client. He filed for divorce on the grounds of adultery and won easily. As I explained earlier, not only was there clear opportunity and inclination here, but the mere fact that the two of them went into a motel room together and stayed more than an hour would have been sufficient. My record of the surveillance and the pictures provided all the documentation that was needed.

When you record a surveillance, be sure your notes are detailed and clear enough to allow you to re-create the scene based on what you've written. Document your movements by making note of cars, license numbers, people, stores, or landmarks. Also record dates and times. Note if there are doormen, parking attendants, or other building employees around because they can provide time-frame reference.

SURVEILLANCE ON FOOT

You still see the following scenes in movies and on TV. The first takes places in a static situation. There is a guy sitting in the hotel lobby reading the newspaper. He is about as inconspicuous as a flashing neon sign. The subject comes in, and the snoop lowers his paper. The subject looks over, and the paper comes up to cover the face. When the subject heads for the elevator, the snoop folds his paper, tucks it under his arm, and follows the guy right into the elevator. The elevator stops at the seventeenth floor and they both get out. The subject goes to room 1709, and the snoop walks on by toward the end of the corridor. Nothing to it.

The second scene occurs on the street. The tail waits on the street corner leaning on the side of a building. He picks up his subject outside an office building and begins to follow him. The subject stops to look into a store window, and the tail stops and takes a long look at his fingernails. This continues for five minutes, with the tail occasionally ducking into a doorway to escape the wary glance of the subject. Finally, the subject goes into a department store, the tail gets bumped by another shopper and knocks some packages to the floor, an argument ensues, and when the tail looks up, the subject has disappeared.

Is it as easy to follow someone in real life without getting burned as it is in fiction? Almost as easy—if you know how. The same rules apply to surveillance on foot that apply to surveillance in a car. You have to stay close enough to keep the person in sight and far enough away so he can't tell he is being followed.

One ploy I've found very useful in a foot surveillance is a dog. Put a dog on a leash and you've got carte blanche. People almost never look at the dog's owner because they are so interested in the dog. They may want to avoid it or hug it, but the dog gets all the attention. In a car surveillance a dog is also useful for the same reasons. I don't know why, but people think a person and his dog are entitled to be anywhere, and that whatever they are doing is above reproach.

As I said, it is obviously a lot easier for a professional investigator to follow a stranger than it is for a husband, wife, friend, or business associate to follow someone who knows her or him. On a crowded street it isn't too difficult to remain out of sight, but in a store or on a street in a residential area it is more difficult. Here are two rules of thumb: 1) on a crowded street, stay on the same side as your subject; and 2) on an uncrowded street, stay on the opposite side. In either case try to walk at roughly the same pace as your subject, stay out of his natural sight lines, and stay back as far as possible but at least fifty feet.

As with a car, know what your subject looks like from the rear so you can quickly identify him in a group of people. Pay special attention to clothes, and make special note of one particular item of clothing such as a hat, a scarf, a large pocket book, a hunting jacket, and so forth. If you find you're having trouble keeping contact on a crowded street, close the gap, but remember that it is better to lose the subject than to be identified.

To minimize the possibility of identification wear different clothing than you normally wear. If you never wear a hat, then wear a hat. If you don't wear glasses, put some on. Again, wear clothes that blend in with the people around you—neither too flashy nor too drab, too fashionable or too unfashionable.

A trick I like to use in a foot surveillance can be employed when you know the final destination of your subject. Instead of following along behind, I will get in front of the person, even arrive at the destination before he does. When was the last time you heard of someone looking for a tail in front of them? It just isn't something that enters people's minds. When a person says, "I think someone is following us," do you look in front of you? No, you look behind, of course. That suspicious-looking guy in front of you couldn't be following you. You can imagine the conversation. "Honey, do you think that man in front of us is following us?" "Don't be silly, love, how could he be following us? He's in front of us." On this same point, an inventor came to my office one day with his brainstorm—a pair of glasses with rearview mirrors. Not a bad idea at first blush, but trying to use them makes your eyeballs spin and gives you a terrific headache. At any rate, following from in front, doing the unexpected, is a tactic that works extremely well.

When you've arrived at your destination (either by being the first one there or arriving after your subject) you have to follow the same methods of documenting your presence that I used in the motel example. Watch as the subjects enter the house or apartment but remember that just because they enter a building doesn't mean they entered a specific apartment. If you don't know for a fact that one of them has an apartment there or that they are using the apartment of a friend, you will have to establish the fact by following them in and noting the floor and apartment they enter. This isn't easy, and I don't recommend it for the amateur.

What I do recommend is that you back off and reassess the situation. One of your alternatives is to check the *Cole's Directory* (see research chapter) for the names of all the people who live at that address. In that listing you may find the name of someone you know your subject knows. Another is to wait until the cosubject comes out, get a good description of that person, and then go through the process of asking questions in the immediate neighborhood. You can pretend to be looking for an heir or a witness to an accident, and in that way pinpoint the location of the apartment. In the suburbs, the *Cole's Directory* is even more useful because you can easily find the resident of a one- or two-family house. And finally, the post office will usually give out the name of the person living at a given address and the local tax collector's office has a listing of property tax payers by address.

I prefer to know in advance where my subjects are headed anyway. It makes for a much more effective, and simpler, investigation. Also remember that you have to prove they are in that apartment alone and you can do it by phone, as I suggested earlier. This means calling before they get there and then again after they've arrived. When you call don't just hang up. A hang-up is a dead giveaway that something strange is going on. So disguise your voice and ask for someone, anyone will do. The answer will verify that your subjects are there. The fact that you saw them go upstairs and verified their presence alone in the place is enough. Then you can wait for them to come out. You don't need to take pictures, but as I've said, pictures are the icing on the cake.

8

Negligence: "So Sue Me!"

The answer is, "Everyone." What is the question? The question is: "How many people in this country know someone who has been involved in a negligence case or have been involved in one themselves?"

Whether it's a fall on the street, a car accident, a product liability case, or a question of malpractice, there isn't a soul left in America who doesn't have firsthand knowledge of a negligence case either as a friend or relative of the plaintiff or defendant, or as an actual participant.

The word "negligence" is a legal term that is applied to those cases where someone sues an individual, a company, a municipality, or a state for damages (either physical or mental or both) incurred through or because of the negligence of the other party. Such a suit makes the accusation that something that one party did or failed to do caused the event, and that damages are due the injured party. In other words, one party has been neglectful or derelict in allowing the event, the accident, to occur.

How many times have we all heard: "I'll sue you for every cent you've got!" The threat to sue seems to be on the tip of everyone's tongue, and the threat is often made to people who don't have a cent to be sued for. I won't even venture a guess as to the number of negligence suits filed in this country each year or to the amount

137

of money involved in settlements and legal fees in this field of the law. But one thing is clear. There is obviously a handsome living to be made by lawyers in negligence cases.

One of the key elements in certain types of negligence cases in New York is that of "prior notice." This means simply that if the person responsible has been notified of a dangerous condition and an accident later occurs because that condition was not remedied after "notice" had been given, the injured party has a right to sue the pants off the responsible person. So, for example, if you have a restriction on your driver's license that says you must drive with glasses and you have an accident, whether it was your fault or not, if you are not wearing your glasses, you have violated the doctrine of prior notice.

Here's a real-life example, a somewhat frightening example, of how prior notice works. As anyone from New York knows, the city has a major problem with potholes in the streets. These potholes, some actually big enough to hold a small car, can and do cause accidents. Cars hit them, go out of control, and break heads. Pedestrians fall in them and break legs. Until a few years ago, when the prior notice concept was instituted, the city was getting sued thousands of times a year by pedestrians, motorists, and cyclists who had negative encounters with potholes. Now the city is only liable in these cases if there has been prior notice about the particular condition and the hole has not been repaired. Not long ago, a group of law firms in the city sent teams of young law students and associates onto the streets and sidewalks of the city to document every pothole and crack in sight so that the city could be put on prior notice in each instance. I'm told that these teams crisscrossed the city like surveyors mapping a new continent and that they measured the depth and width of each and every pothole to the quarter inch. I don't know if a single negligence case developed from this in-depth exploration, but it is certain and verifiable proof that attorneys are not just sitting around on their briefs waiting for business to come in over the transom.

The reason lawyers are eager for these cases is that settlements can be huge, and the lawyer's share can be anywhere from 25 to 50 percent of that settlement. The other reason is that they and their clients bear relatively little expense for bringing the suit in the first place, compared to what they might collect. So in essence the lawyers and the clients have little to lose. The United States is the most litigious country in the world, and one reason is the low cost of filing suit. In many countries the loser must pay the fees in a civil suit—this cuts down tremendously on the number of cases. In their defense, however, let me cite the fact that in this country lawyers collect nothing unless they win. They don't even get reimbursed for their time and expenses, so there is risk involved.

Most of us have what is called "liability" insurance that protects us financially if we are sued for negligence at home, in our offices, or in our cars. I happen to have an umbrella policy that covers me in all three areas, but it's just as easy to have one policy for the car, one for the house, and one for the office. And woe betide the person without it. Your entire future can go down the tubes with one car accident or if someone slips on your floor.

Where does the private investigator come into this picture? Well, the naked truth is that there are a great many negligence suits filed each year that are not quite legitimate. In fact, many are completely fraudulent. Back injuries, which are particularly hard to prove or disprove medically, are the most frequently fabricated physical injuries, but there are hundreds of other minor problems that result in false claims and suits. All it takes is someone slipping on your bathroom floor, and the next thing you know they have a "back injury" and you have a lawsuit on your back.

A number of years ago there was a group of con artists in New York City who made their living by being hit by cars. They were an extremely clever and athletic, even acrobatic, group and they were very enterprising. Their scam worked like this. A team of two men would walk down the street and when the timing was right one of them would step into the street in front of a moving car. It didn't matter if the car was going ten or thirty miles an hour because these guys were good. As soon as the car touched the pedestrian, he would flip himself up over the hood and fall to the street. The whole act was performed with the skill and agility of a movie stuntman. As soon as the victim hit the pavement he would bite into a blood capsule and a trickle of blood would instantly appear at the corner of his mouth. His partner would rush up to the "victim" and start screaming that the driver had killed his friend. The driver, of course, was astonished that someone had run right into his car, and shocked by the apparently serious injury. In the meantime, the victim would slowly come to his senses, clutch his lower back, and moan in mighty pain.

The ambulance would cart the victim off to the hospital, where he'd stay for a week or ten days, and in the meantime the legal papers would be filed. It was all a complete sham, but it cost the insurance companies dearly until the charade was exposed. I didn't work on that case, but I wish I had because it was a fascinating gimmick.

The insurance companies clearly don't want to pay for fake injuries of any kind, and most lawyers don't want to be involved in a phony case either because not only is it bad for their personal reputations and for the image of the profession, but it can prove costly for the lawyer as well. This is where the call goes out to the PI. I'm hired by either the insurance company or the lawyer, and my job is to document the true extent of the injury.

By the way, I don't want you to get the impression that all injuries are phony or that all negligence suits are invalid, only that the possibility of fraud exists and there are always people who will rush in to fill that sort of vacuum.

Recently, I was hired by the lawyer for a health club to determine the extent of the injuries suffered by one of the club's members. The member had filed a negligence suit against the club because he said he had permanently lost most of the movement in his right arm and shoulder when one of the club's weight machines had malfunctioned while he was using it. The guy had a medical report that supported his story and a photo that showed him standing with one shoulder much higher than the other. The club was insured but felt he was exaggerating the extent of the injury and that his claim for $3 million was considerably overblown.

I talked with the man's doctor, who told me that he wasn't sure how immobilizing the injury would be, if at all, but he said it had probably been painful and would take some time to heal. The physical therapist at the club was also uncertain but thought the picture looked a little odd.

What I needed was a picture of the guy with his shirt off that would show that his shoulder really was, or really wasn't, as bad as he claimed. Through his lawyer he refused to let me take a picture, so I set up a photo surveillance in the hope that I'd at least be able to get a shot of him wearing a T-shirt. In this case I got lucky. It was summer, and one hot Saturday morning he came out of his apartment with his little girl and the two of them walked to a small neighborhood park. I took up a position where I could see them clearly and got my camera ready. The man put down a blanket, and while the child sat contentedly, he took off his shirt. I got a dozen good shots and was about to leave when he bent over and picked up his child using both his arms. Then in typical parental fashion he lifted her up over his head and threw her in the air several times. I was snapping away like crazy. He then put her under his arm on the side of the bad shoulder and carried her over to the swings. I took several shots of that and had more than enough. As I left all I could think was that he sure seemed to be a nice father.

With the photos I had, the value of the man's case was lowered considerably. He still won medical and other damages out of court but the entire settlement, instead of $3 million, was less than $30,000. The insurance company and the health club were both pleased.

What happens in many legitimate negligence cases, like the one above, is that the injured party asks for an amount of money that is pumped up bigger than a balloon. What the claimant and his attorney hope is that the case will eventually come before a sympathetic jury. Juries are very generous in this type of case because they can see how the same thing might happen to them in the future. At the very least, the lawyers hope for a large out-of-court settlement because the insurance company is afraid the jury will sympathize with the claimant.

My guess is that least 30 percent of all negligence claims are phony or exaggerated to some degree. It's a big-stakes gambling game and that's why investigators are worth their fees. We're hired to determine the facts and to see if there is liability or contributory negligence on the part of the defendant. The defendant and the insurance company want to make sure the claim is legitimate and within reason.

Of course, the other side of the coin is the absolutely legitimate negligence case, like those where a piece of the ceiling falls on a tenant, a fire escape collapses, facing falls off the front of a building, or a crane topples over into the street.

It may sound strange, but there are a lot of cases where falling ceilings are involved and if there is an injury in a ceiling case the landlord and insurance company are both dead, even if the injured party is not.

In a case I handled a few years ago, the claim was that the bathroom ceiling fell on a woman while she was brushing her teeth. It was said that a large piece of plaster hit her on the head and knocked her unconscious. She was not injured critically but she was cut and bleeding. She was found on the floor of the bathroom by her daughter who had heard the noise and rushed in to see what had happened. The daughter immediately called an ambulance and went with her mother to the hospital where the mother was admitted, treated, and released three days later.

In this case there was no question about the ceiling falling, but the woman's attorney hired me to document the fact that she had been in the bathroom at the time and had not rushed in after the plaster fell to lie there and appear injured. I got statements from the woman and her daughter, but the proof was in the statement I took from one of the ambulance drivers. He said that when he got there the old woman was still unconscious and she had plaster in her hair and toothpaste in her mouth. These small facts clinched the case, and the woman won a substantial settlement.

The legitimate stairway fall is also a typical negligence case, the kind that anyone could be involved in because, as we've all heard since childhood, more accidents happen in the home than anywhere else. Let's say Cousin Stan falls down the steps in his apartment building and breaks his hip. He says that he tripped over a loose piece of carpet on the second step and that he had also tripped on the same spot while going down the stairs a few weeks earlier. He also says that he wrote the landlord a letter complaining about the carpet and demanding that the stairway be repaired "before someone really gets hurt."

My investigation of this type of case would involve a statement from the victim and a copy of his letter to the landlord. I would then do the kind of detailed and painstaking documentation that may put you to sleep while you're reading about it but is, nevertheless, absolutely essential when it comes to winning or losing a case. Here are the facts that you need to find out:

- How many steps are there?
- What are they made of (wood, marble, tile); are they carpeted; is the carpet in good repair?
- What is the depth and height of each step? Is one step an inch or two higher or lower than the others?
- What is the lighting like? Natural and/or artificial, fluorescent or regular, covered or uncovered? What is the wattage?
- Are the handrails attached to the wall or to the steps? Are they firmly attached (shake the railing)? What is the distance from the step to the top of the railing?
- Is there nosing on the steps and is it raised or flush?

The reason for this careful documentation is that there are building codes that standardize most of these elements, and if the landlord or the builder is in violation of the code he is in trouble. If there has been a prior accident, that fact usually weighs devastatingly in favor of the plaintiff. And in this example, the prior notice given by Cousin Stan is also critical. If a neighbor had fallen instead, Stan's letter would still have served as prior notice. At the time you have an accident you may not know if there has been prior notice of the condition, but it is the first thing you should find out.

Falls of all kinds commonly result in negligence suits. I had a case where a woman fell on the floor of a butcher shop and badly injured her back, for real. She was rushed to the hospital by ambulance, had surgery, and spent more than two months recuperating in the hospital and another six months in traction at home.

She claimed she had slipped on a puddle of water that had accumulated on the floor of the shop. I was working for her lawyer so I was looking for evidence or the testimony of witnesses that there had been water on the floor at the time of her fall. I talked at length with the butchers (who were fully insured) and the four other people who had been in the store at the time of the accident.

None of them had noticed any water on the floor and there had been no complaints from customers earlier in the day.

I talked to the victim again, and she swore to me that there was water and that it was the cause of her fall. I then talked with the ambulance driver and asked if he or his partner had noticed any water on the floor. He said no. Then I asked if the victim's dress had been wet when they picked her up to put her on the stretcher. The driver thought for a moment and said that he had noticed a large wet spot on her dress but had thought nothing of it at the time.

What had happened was simple. There had been water, the women had slipped on it, and when she fell she fell in the water, which was absorbed into her dress. When she was carried away there was no evidence left. This may sound a little like Sherlock Holmes, but that's the way it happened and she won a very large claim, which made my client, the lawyer, very happy.

By far the most common kind of negligence case, however, is the one that stems from an auto accident. With few exceptions, one driver is always considered negligent in a car crash. The police are usually involved in the investigation in auto cases, but here is some advice that will help you help them and yourself if you're in an accident.

- Try to keep cool.
- Get the names, addresses, and telephone numbers of witnesses on the street.
- Get the license plate numbers of the cars around, because they may well drive off.
- Keep a cheap camera with a flash in the glove compartment: a picture is worth a thousand words. Take pictures of the scene, the cars, the skid marks.

I suppose I've investigated a thousand auto accident cases over the years and most of them are just a matter of piecing together the facts from the drivers, the passengers, the police, and the witnesses. Usually, it is tedious legwork.

But occasionally there is a case with a twist. I had such a case where two drivers were each claiming negligence on the part of the other, but no one was sure how the accident had really happened. The two cars had collided at a major intersection where a policeman was directing traffic at the time. It seemed to be a question of who had the right of way, but more was involved. One driver was headed north and the other east but both told the same story. They both stopped at the corner because the traffic signal was not working. They both saw the cop in the middle of the street and they looked to him for a signal. He was using hand signals and he seemed to direct both cars to go ahead at the same time. They collided in the middle of the intersection, just missing the cop. One of the drivers told me it was like an old-time movie with the Keystone Kops deciding it's "let's have an accident time." Both drivers sued, but the case was finally dropped because neither could prove negligence, neither had been injured, and the city paid for the auto repairs.

Accidents in vehicles other than private cars are also quite common. Here the same rules apply (except for the camera), because you will have to prove the facts in order to file a claim. If you should fall and injure yourself on a train or bus, you'll have to document the fact that "suddenly, and without warning, the bus lurched and several people fell to the floor." You need the names and addresses of those people, the name of the bus driver, the bus ID number, the route, the time of day, the location of "the lurch," and any other information you can get. Witnesses are really the most important factor in this kind of situation because the burden of proof is on you. You have to do the proving, and witnesses provide the proof.

Since witnesses are so important, it is critical that you know the proper way to take a statement from a witness. This isn't done at the scene of the accident, but it should be done as soon as possible after the fact so that the person's memory of the situation is still clear.

I tell you honestly that there are very few people, including experienced policemen, who take good, solid, well-documented statements. It may be a little boastful, but I happen to be one of those people.

Here are the rules I follow:

• Identify the statement with the day, month, year, time of day taken, and place taken.

• Include full name—first, middle, and last, and any nicknames.

• Take vital statistics—age, marital status, date of birth, Social Security number, address, city, state, apartment number, length of time at that address, and if there less than three years include the previous address, home phone with area code, place employed with address, city, state, and phone with area code.

• Spell everything in full, for example: age twenty-five (25); Rochester, New York.

• Be definitive—give date of the accident or incident, day of week, approximate time within five minutes, location at time of accident, what corner, why there, weather at the time.

• Number each line of the statement. Just where the statement ends, have the person place his initials. Below that have him write in his own hand, "I have read the above three pages, sixty-eight lines, and understand each and every line, and it is true."

• Don't try to take shortcuts.

There are two other areas of negligence—product liability and malpractice—and entire books have been written on each subject. Neither of these negligence situations is easy to prove, but the rules of the game are the same. You have to do all the legwork, talk to all the players, take statements, and in general, conduct the investigation in the same manner as any other investigation. What you have to do is prove that the product or service was at fault and that you have suffered some loss through the negligence of the company or the individual.

Here are two examples. Years ago, when I was an investigator for an insurance company, we were sued by a man who claimed he found a large bug in his soft-drink bottle. This kind of incident brings thoughts of lawsuits and huge settlements, but such a claim is always open to question. In this case the claimant was asking for a lot of money and my job was to prove that he had not suffered any harm.

First, I checked the store where the bottle was purchased. It was a reputable place that had no record of problems with the health department. Then I went to the distributor. Here again, no problems. The suit claimed the bottle had been partially open so I questioned the people who were with him at the time. No one remembered the bottle being open. He did not get sick and rush to the hospital, though several days later he did go to his personal doctor and he had a bill to prove it. I checked to see if the man had a history of making such claims, but this was apparently his first. If he had drunk from the bottle and gotten sick that would have been important, but he apparently discovered the bug before drinking and that's a soda of another flavor. Using the results of my investigation, our lawyer contacted the claimant's lawyer and the whole matter was settled for the amount of the doctor bill.

Then there are situations where you will need to prove negligence. Let's say you buy a ladder to do some repair work on your ceiling. You set the ladder up properly and begin to climb in order to make your repairs. When you get to the fourth rung, it collapses and you fall heavily to the floor and break your leg. You very likely have a legitimate product liability claim, but you still have to prove it.

You should go to the store where you bought the ladder and ask if they have had any problems. Call the company and ask them the same thing. You can hire an engineer who will test the bearing weight of the ladder's rungs and advise you of any federal regulations that apply to the manufacture of ladders. With your findings, and a report from your doctor and the hospital emergency room, you're ready to file your claim.

The guiding principle is simple: The product you buy must be safe and workable. If it is a service, you are entitled to safe and successful treatment. But the burden of proof in any case is on the person claiming damages. A loss must be proved. I should point out, however, that the medical establishment and large corporations are not quite as vulnerable as the health club and the butcher shop and therefore your documentation will need to be as detailed and accurate as you can possibly get it.

9

Wills and Estates: A Question of Competence and Undue Influence

I mentioned earlier that domestic cases are statistically the most dangerous for the police because emotions run high and the potential for physical violence is always in the air. Well, when it comes to the battle over a will and the division of an estate, emotions also run high because money and property are involved and occasionally the family honor as well. And though the courts and lawyers are usually prominent in the picture, and the legal proceedings, meetings, and negotiations may be conducted in a more civilized manner, the potential for violent disagreement is high when an estate is being decided.

During the time when a will is being probated, it's not uncommon for brother to verbally threaten or physically attack brother, for the first wife to pull the second wife by the hair, and for both of them to castigate the third wife, for children to scream epithets at parents, even for entire families to split up, never to speak to each other again. I've seen it all.

And what is truly amazing to me is that the warring parties are often arguing over as little as $500, a piece of furniture that's worth perhaps $25, or the title to some swampland that never has been and never will be worth anything. The very fact that people will fight over something like a piece of furniture, a painting, a rug, a pet, a TV set, or an old car is beyond my comprehension.

Petty and nasty are two of the nicer words that can be used to describe the situation. In my experience, the amount of money spent on the fees of private investigators and attorneys in many estate cases often exceeds the value of the money or property that precipitated the quarrel.

I'd be willing to bet that many of you have been involved in such situations and know what I'm saying is true, but for those of you who haven't, let me give you an example that illustrates what I'm talking about and that highlights many of the major issues in estate cases.

At the time, this case received a lot of attention from the New York media. Night after night there was a story on the television news and every day the papers expanded on what the TV news had to say. The decedent in this case was a seventy-seven-year-old woman living alone in a large house in a wealthy Long Island community not far from the fashionable beaches of Southampton. She had been widowed for more than twenty years and had been living as a semirecluse for much of that time. Her husband, a wealthy scrap metal dealer, had left her a good deal of money, and on the surface it appeared that she had spent very little of it.

Normally, no one would have paid much attention to her but in her later years she had become known locally as the Cat Lady because she collected stray cats. Neighbors had reported her to the health department several times because of the number of cats in and around her house and the potential health hazard the cats posed to the neighborhood. The police were called in when the woman was found dead one morning by her twice-a-week house-keeper. When the police responded to the maid's frantic call they found the body (it had been there for three days) and more than fifty cats on the premises. There was no evidence of robbery or any kind of struggle or foul play, and the death was termed natural.

In their report the police also said that despite the apparent ef-forts of the maid, the house was filthy and a complete shambles inside—fifty cats can do that, I suppose—and that according to the maid, the woman lived on virtually nothing, sometimes eating cat food herself. So though her children suspected she had money, appearances would lead one to think that she was indigent. Her children, two sons and a daughter, had not been in close touch with her and seemed to have no idea of her living conditions.

The police found two wills in a strongbox in the woman's bedroom. One was dated at the time of her husband's death and called for an equal division of her assets among her three children. The second, dated only one year before her death and consequently the one in force, called for a bequest of $250,000 to her maid, $5,000 to each of the three children, and left the remainder to the Society for the Prevention of Cruelty to Animals on Long Island and to a religious organization she had belonged to many years before.

I was asked into the case by the oldest daughter because she felt sure her mother had gone bonkers somewhere in the last year or she wouldn't have signed such a ridiculous will. The daughter cited the condition of the house and the cats as evidence, and she felt the second will must have been made by an incompetent. Since her mother's circumstances didn't appear prosperous, the daughter didn't know whether or not there was anything of substance to divide in the estate, even though large amounts were mentioned. But she was certain that her mother was not in her right mind when she made out the second will and that she and her two brothers were entitled to share in the estate, whatever it finally amounted to.

A few days later, the Cat Lady's case made really big news, national news, after a meeting between the daughter and the decedent's lawyer, who told her that according to his calculations, the estate was worth upward of $11 million. The mother had lived austerely, but her husband's investments had done very well indeed. Clearly there was now likely to be a healthy inheritance for the SPCA and the religious group, if not for the children. Believe me, I've seen knockdown battles over much less, so this promised to be a big event.

There are usually two major questions in this type of case: the competency of the decedent at the time the will was made, and/or whether there was undue influence exerted on the person at the time the will was made. Both incompetence (harboring fifty stray cats seems a bit strange) and undue influence (considering the size of the bequest to the maid) were possibilities in this case. The daughter hired me to determine whether either or both of these situations existed at the time the second will was signed.

The daughter believed I would find that her mother was not

competent or had been influenced. From what the daughter told me, and from what I knew from the news, I felt she might be right on target, but as I've said before, my job isn't to judge, only to go to work.

In any case, proving incompetence is a tricky thing. The discoveries I make about a person's actions, habits, or idiosyncrasies are not conclusive evidence of incompetence or anything else. They do, however, represent the parts of a puzzle that may eventually prove a case of incompetence.

The problem is that what may seem to be an odd set of actions to some people may be part of a person's natural makeup. If your brother Steve likes to sit on the porch in boxer shorts and rubber boots, that isn't a sign that he is of failing mind. Your grandma Bett may eat with her fingers, drink water with a spoon, send get-well cards to strangers, and watch television until 3:00 A.M. These eccentricities may simply be part of her character. But if you add these things together you may come up with a total that is more than the sum of the parts.

The physical problems that accompany old age are not proof of incompetence either. An eighty-year-old man who can't sign his name firmly may just be exhibiting the infirmity of age, not suffering from some debilitating illness that is affecting his mind. Such aging problems as halting speech, poor hearing, and problems walking are perfectly normal signs of deteriorating health. It's mostly the thought processes that I need to confirm when I investigate in a competence case, because it is the state of the mind and not the state of the body that the court will use to make its determination.

Proving undue influence is also complex. There have been many cases where a young housekeeper or nurse has been written into a will for a large percentage of the estate of the man she had been caring for. In such cases the wife and the children are usually left bequests but not what they consider their fair share. Though the deceased may be proved competent, the investigation may show that he was influenced by the nurse or housekeeper, especially by the ministrations of a pretty woman thirty or forty years his junior.

Some of these cases have turned on whether the woman—or male companion of a woman—influenced the change in a will with the deceased unaware of how he was being influenced. For example, if the person who takes care of you every day makes casual comments like, "My daughter would never treat me that way," or "Why doesn't your son come to see you more often," or "I overheard your daughter-in-law saying nasty things about you," what's an old man to think? These are subtle ways of changing a person's thinking, ways that can have a cumulative effect over a period of months or years, and can result in changes in wills.

In influence cases I watch for the late arrivals in a person's life—new lawyers, girlfriends, housekeepers, or wives. Those May-December marriages are not always beautiful romances based on true love and affection. Some people make a career out of becoming heirs in much the same way people make a career out of having accidents. For this reason I always check to see if the unexpected heir has been left money in similar instances in the past. For me, the person's background and the amount of time the person has been on the scene are critical information.

And keep this in mind as well. The questions of competence and undue influence cut both ways. If you are the heir to a will, the big inheritor, and someone challenges the competence of the deceased or the amount of influence you brought to bear on the person, you are going to want to prove the deceased's competence and freedom from influence. If the shoe is on the other foot you will interpret the deceased's actions quite differently. I've had cases where brothers and sisters, one having received more than the other, have fought over the inheritance, both hiring private investigators. It would be funny if it wasn't tragic. On one side you have an heir trying to prove competence and on the other side a member of the family trying to prove incompetence.

But back to the example. Here is what I did in the case of the Cat Lady.

I always like to go after the question of competence first, because it is easier to prove or disprove than undue influence, so my first job was to talk to the family lawyer. He had not been involved in writing the second will, but he did have regular contact with the decedent because he sent her a monthly check from the estate and spoke with her from time to time on the telephone. He told me that in his opinion, except for her obsession with stray cats, she had been of sound mind at the time of her death. He had also reviewed the second will when it was discovered and felt it was a perfectly valid legal document with valid signatures, witnesses, dates, and seals.

Next I had to locate the two witnesses to the second will and interview them. I wanted to validate their signatures but I also wanted to talk to them about the mental state of the Cat Lady at the time she formulated and promulgated the second will. Their opinions would be valuable.

How do you judge the competence of someone? There are a number of indicators that go into the formula.

For example, how did the person act? A person may be reclusive and private like the Cat Lady, moderately active and visible in the community, or very social. A person may appear in public acting the way we (and the courts) consider normal, or they may do eccentric things, like talk to themselves or yell epithets at strangers.

How did the person appear—neat and well groomed, dirty and slovenly, or somewhere in between?

Did the person do what might be considered odd things? I once had an estate case in which the decedent regularly met callers at his house wearing a Halloween mask and gave presents wrapped in toilet paper to total strangers.

Did the person manage his or her own money and checking account? Was he able to go to the bathroom by himself, or feed himself? Was he lucid in conversation and able to read a newspaper?

The people that can give you this information are family members, maids, nurses, friends, neighbors, mailmen, insurance agents, grocery clerks, other merchants, and anyone else who might have had regular contact with the deceased. Doctors are worth a try, though they usually won't be much help. The fire department and the police department can be good sources, because a person who is mentally incompetent often calls these agencies on a regular basis. It isn't unusual for a mentally incompetent older person to turn in false alarms or to badger the police with all manner of complaints.

In one of my cases, the decedent called the fire department at least twice a week to report a roaring blaze in her kitchen. In another case, a father hired me to determine if his forty-year-old son should be committed to a mental institution. I was never able to find any valid grounds for commitment despite the fact that one of the things the son did was call the police precinct in his neighborhood as many as forty times a week every week for four years complaining about the noise his neighbors were making. The kicker was that he was nearly deaf, so the noise of the neighbors was in his head. But even the police, who were being driven crazy by these calls, couldn't get the poor man committed to an institution.

The neighbors can be especially helpful in competence cases because a person's response to his or her neighbors can indicate mental instability. For example, if the man next door, the one who has been growling at you and your kids for years, suddenly becomes an angel and offers the kids sugar cookies, he may have a mental problem. By the same token, if the nice little white-haired lady down the block with the sweet little dog suddenly buys a Doberman and sics him on the kids next door, there is probably a loose wire somewhere. So if people are as surly as ever or as nice as ever, there is little reason to believe that they are incompetent.

Eating habits can offer important clues to competence, and drug usage can be a major influence on a person's ability to act in a competent manner. Quirks, if they do exist, must form a pattern, not just be one-time or occasional things. And be careful not to latch onto something that is not really irrational.

But I've digressed again. The bank told me that the Cat Lady continued to sign her own checks and showed me the last check they had received. The "degree of penmanship" on a check or other signed document shows competency. The firmness and steadiness of the signature and correct spelling are indicative, but any minor changes could just be a sign of physical age. We all change our way of writing through the years. A look back at old signatures or handwritten materials will give a standard of comparison. A handwriting analyst can be called in to help make these determinations, but that isn't often necessary. In this case the Cat Lady's signatures were all firm and easy to read. There had been no unusual withdrawals and nothing to indicate a greater level of spending than normal.

This indicated to me that the woman was more than likely capable of making a new will or twenty new wills if she felt like it, and I saw no reason to pursue the incompetence question. This meant that only proof of undue influence would change the will to benefit my client.

The bequest of money or property to a lifelong companion is not necessarily a questionable act; in fact, it is quite common. It only becomes questionable in the light of investigation. In the course of my investigation into the competency issue I had also asked the banker, the merchants, and the neighbors about the maid. This produced almost no information because she seemed to have one job and that was to come twice a week and try and clean up the mess made by all those cats. She didn't sign checks, she didn't shop, she didn't even chat with the neighbors, and the Cat Lady's children had never met her.

Neither had I, so I went to her house to talk with her about her business and personal relationship with the deceased. The woman lived with her husband in a modest house in a small town about a half-hour drive from the Cat Lady's home. She told me she had worked for the woman for three years, had always found her pleasant to be around, and that she had always been paid in cash for her work. She told me she had no idea that a will even existed, let alone that she was included in it. In my estimation she was telling the truth. I judged her to be a rather timid person and not the type of person who would be capable of applying undue influence to anyone, including her own children. It was a straightforward, honest interview. I thanked her and left with the distinct feeling that everything she told me was the truth and the bequest was only made because the Cat Lady liked the maid and possibly felt sorry for her less than handsome circumstances.

The maid had given me the names of two other women she worked for and I talked with them the next day. Both were well-to-do and both said the same thing—that the maid was reliable, prompt, a hard worker, and absolutely honest. Neither woman had ever noticed anything missing from her home, and they both said that they had no qualms about leaving the maid alone in the house while she was working. One of them told me she had read about the case in the paper and that she couldn't see how the maid could have forced the deceased to do anything. And she cited as evidence the fact that the maid had tried to refuse a Christmas bonus because she was too proud to accept money for work that she had not done.

As far as I was concerned the case was closed. I met with the daughter to tell her my findings, and I handed her a report that summarized the results of my investigation. She was not happy with those results, and I later heard that she went to another private investigator and had the job done all over again. The results were apparently the same because the judge ultimately ruled that the will was valid and the funds were distributed as the Cat Lady had desired.

Over the years, I've found the courts to be eminently fair in estate cases, and I think the judges try to operate in the best interests of all the parties. Even in a case like this, where the will was made while the person was competent and there is no valid way to break it, the court may make some small changes at the discretion of the judge.

In estate cases I try to keep in mind that senility is a much overworked word. Most older people aren't senile at all, though their heirs would like to think they are. In fact, many older people are tough as nails and the wills they forge, even in their later years, are well thought out and airtight.

Every family will eventually be involved in an estate situation. When it is your turn, if you have reason to believe that the deceased was incompetent or unduly influenced, you can try and break that will. A PI can cost a lot of money but you can now save most of that money by doing some, or all, of the work yourself.

10

The Drug Problem

One other type of investigation in which I find myself involved is family-oriented drug cases, that is, cases in which parents hire me to determine if their kid is using drugs and where the kid is getting the stuff. I must admit I'm a bit reluctant to accept these cases because I think parents are capable of handling them better than I am, and I have the feeling that hiring an investigator is often a way of avoiding the problem rather than confronting it. But I said I'm not judgmental, and so I take on these cases as I do all the rest. With drugs such a big part of life in this country today, you may run into the problem in your own family, and you may want to investigate the situation on your own. Here are some things that you should know.

Drugs are all over—in the best of homes and the worst; among the best of kids and the worst. And despite the fact that drug abuse by teenagers is one of the biggest problems facing American society today, drugs are apparently here to stay. Experts in the field tell me that in the future the flow of drugs may be controlled to a certain extent, but that the flow may never be stopped. This is a sobering thought and one that parents of young and teenage children must confront. One way to do this is to make yourself aware of the effects of drugs on a person and familiarize yourself with where drugs are available.

First, here are some telltale signs of drug use. Be alert for these signs because they usually indicate trouble:

- Sleeping ten, twelve, fourteen hours a day or more
- Staying home from school or work
- Items missing from the home and from relatives' homes
- Unusual behavior, that is, changes in behavior patterns
- Wild swings in mood
- Sudden, unprovoked anger

The following scenario will give you an idea of how these signs show up in the normal course of events.

Scene One

Parent: Mary, you seem to be sleeping a lot lately. Do you feel all right?
Mary: Sure, Mom, I'm fine. Just a little tired, that's all. I've been working hard at school, you know.

Extra hours of sleep and drowsiness when awake are two of the major indicators of drug use.

Scene Two

Parent: Mary, I left some money in the dresser drawer and it's not there. Did you borrow it?
Mary: No, Mom, honest. You must have spent it. What do I need money for?

Taking money from parents, brothers, and sisters in order to pay for drugs and pills and then denying the fact is a common occurrence when a teenager starts to use drugs.

Scene Three

Parent: Mary, Aunt Irene just called and asked if you'd seen her gold chain when you were visiting last Sunday. Did you see it?
Mary: Mom, what do you think I am, a thief? For God's sake, don't you trust your own child?

Increasing the ante—in other words, taking things from the homes of relatives and even friends—is another step along the drug road. When the need for money is severe, youngsters often resort to stealing from the homes and apartments of strangers. Parents and relatives aren't likely to have their own kin arrested, but strangers won't hesitate.

SCENE FOUR

Parent: I found these pills in your room and these marijuana cigarettes in your schoolbag. What's going on here?

Mary: Oh, Mom, those aren't mine, I'm just keeping them for a friend.

Parent: What friend?

Mary: I can't tell you.

Parent: I think we'd better figure out what's going on here.

Outright lying by a child is one of the final steps in this relatively short road to heavy drug use.

SCENE FIVE

Mary: OK, I admit I was taking pills and smoking grass, and I swear I'll never do it again, OK? Just leave me alone.

Parent: I'm not going to leave you alone until we take care of the problem. You're going to see the doctor, and we're going to find out what to do.

The admission of drug use is a step in the right direction. At this point it's up to the child and the parent to seek professional answers. Those answers may be found in a drug program, private counseling or therapy, or group counseling, but it is clear that in this type of case drastic action must be taken.

Direct action is the right course, but don't kid yourself. Drug use is a hard thing to control because drugs are available everywhere. They can be purchased on the street corner, in the bar, in the park, and around—and in—the school.

The following example is all too common. I was called by parents who felt their teenage son was involved in drugs. They live in an affluent suburb of Philadelphia, and the boy was attending a fancy private school with children from some of the best families in the area. They had checked with other parents and, though some of their friends suspected trouble, no one was certain, primarily because they couldn't figure out where the kids would get drugs in that area. After all, there were no pushers hanging out on the corner.

From previous experience, I strongly suspected that the school was unwittingly involved, so I arranged for a young-looking operative of mine to act the role of a new student in the school. My man found that drugs—marijuana, cocaine, heroin, hashish, and various types of pills—were being sold daily at one specific table in the cafeteria. There was a steady stream of business at that table and the school authorities were apparently ignorant of the fact or had chosen to overlook it. My man was able to obtain the names of the kids who held office hours at that table, and I took my information to the parents who hired me. Along with a group of concerned parents, they then presented the facts to the headmaster, and those students directly involved with the selling were arrested.

The point is, there is almost no way to prevent a child from getting drugs if the desire is there. Of course, the more money the child has, the easier it is for him or her to get the goods. Drug education programs can be useful, but only fast action can help once the problem exists.

You should also know that anyone addicted to drugs is a "junkie," whether living at home or on the streets, and in fact most teenage junkies are not on the streets. They still live comfortably with the family. But be aware that the life of the junkie is not a pleasant one even with the comforts of home. If lucky, he or she wakes up in the morning to find a little bit of stash left from the night before. It may be enough to keep him or her going for a while. But then these junkies have to get more, and if they don't have money they have to go out on the street to shoplift, break into cars, apartments, and houses, snatch purses, and find any other way they can to get money.

When a drug habit is advanced, stealing is a necessity. Once the stolen property is in hand, the junkie has to find somebody to buy it and that means "offing" it to a fence, a person who is a buyer of stolen property. Now that the junkie has a little bit of money, he or she has to find a connection (the source of drugs) and hope that the merchandise is available. The junkie then has to find some place to smoke, shoot up, snort, or pop pills. Depending on the size of the junkie's habit, this pattern may have to be repeated several times a day, every day, with no Sundays off.

Admittedly, this is not a pretty picture, and I'm presenting these details only because I think it helps to clarify the ultimate danger of drug use. How many kids resort to crime to support their habit? In the beginning, probably none. When the habit increases, many of them have to steal to pay the piper. Stealing, however, is a dangerous business, since eventually only two things can happen: you can get caught by the victim, or you can get caught by the police.

Despite the abundance and immediate availability of drugs, it is my experience that parents always find it hard to believe that their child is using drugs. They say, "No, not my kid." But after I've verified the facts for them, they know they must act, and most parents do act. The problem is, if the kids using the drugs aren't interested in helping themselves, even if they spend five hundred hours with the best psychiatrist in the world it isn't going to help. They must want help. Finding the source of drugs probably won't do much good because the user will find someone else. There is no stopping the junkie who needs drugs. And don't think that pills are not addictive, or less of a problem, because they are. In many ways pills are more dangerous than other drugs. A kid will pop one pill and feel a little something but not enough. He'll take another and then two more and pretty soon he's walking through a plate glass window or driving his car into a tree.

My advice to parents is to be very alert. Don't shrug off behavior and excuses that you want to believe. At the first sign of trouble, look into it. If you sweep it under the rug, it may be too late by the time you're ready to do something about it. And don't be put off by promises. A drug user will promise you the world. He'll say, "I won't do it anymore," "I'll pay you back," "I'll go back to school," "I'll get a job." Don't believe it. Present the facts to the youngster and take a firm stance. Err on the side of caution. Be firm. I'd rather hurt the kid's feelings than see him go under, because he is surely going to die—killed by drugs, in a holdup, or in jail.

11

Info. 101: How to Research Your Subject

When I was in school, the words "term paper" used to strike fear and loathing into my heart. To me a term paper symbolized restricted hours in my favorite tavern drinking beer and unrestricted, seemingly endless hours of research in the library poring over, around, and through reference books, encyclopedias, and volumes of dry information that I would plagiarize once and never use again. I mean how many times in this life do we need to know enough to write forty pages on the causes of the Civil War?

So when I finished my last term paper in the last semester of my senior year in college I breathed a deep sigh of relief because I was certain I'd never have to go through that kind of hell again.

Then I became an insurance investigator and the first thing I learned was that my days of research had only just begun. Sure, it wasn't quite the same because my insurance work served a real purpose, but I was involved in serious research that required me to pore over, around, and through material that might never be useful to me again. But I applied myself. I got my training on the job, and I learned how to do it right.

The correct methods and procedures of research were skills I had to learn because some degree of research is required in virtually every case a private investigator handles. In fact, the first steps I take in many cases are in the direction of the library or the courthouse, and these first steps usually provide the leads that I use to pursue that case to its conclusion.

In the old days, of course, "research" was called by a less fancy name—it was referred to as "legwork." Today, with the help of the computer it can become "fingerwork." Nevertheless, most of my research still requires the investigator to apply foot to pavement instead of fingers to keyboard. No matter what method is used or what it's called, research is a vital part of my business.

But there is a marked difference between my kind of research and the kind done by the academic researcher who spends most of his or her time in the library in a solitary hunt for facts. While my research often begins at the library, most of it is conducted with people who control information. The results I achieve are dependent on how well I handle, you might even say manipulate, those people. The time I do spend in the library is rarely back in the stacks with the history majors. Most of my research is done in public and at any or all of the following levels:

- City
- County
- State
- Federal
- International

Each of these levels can yield vast amounts of data on people, places, and things, and it is a rare case that doesn't involve considerable digging in more than one of these areas.

I said I depend on people in my research, so before I give you concrete examples of how to work at each of the levels mentioned above, let me give you a little warning about working with people. It's a fact of the private investigator's life and work that a good deal of our research is conducted in and through various government offices. Government offices contain huge mountains of information, and those mountains must be mined. I have spent untold hours, by now they probably add up to years, in those pale green surroundings, and there have been many times when frustration caused by the inefficiency, uncooperativeness, and incompetence of some government functionaries has turned my face a contrasting bright red and a gorge has risen in my throat.

I've found government agencies to be much like the army. There is a whole lot of waiting involved. To pass the waiting time I've read, I've slept, I've done crossword puzzles, I've cut my fingernails, I've wept, while the agents of my frustration sit calmly behind their desks and go through their maddening charades. I've borne witness to coffee breaks, lunches, birthday parties, retirement celebrations, and funerals. What I've rarely borne witness to is work.

In other words, I have experience in dealing with bureaucracies, and I have the scars that allow me to speak with authority. So, back to the warning. Over the years, I have developed a working hypothesis and this is it: There is a thing that exists out there in government offices. It's there just beyond the outer fringes of our imagination and consciousness, a thing that affects the mind, a thing so horrible that most of us can't look it in the face for more than a few seconds. What is this horror, the monster that roams at will through all our government offices? It's called "the civil service mentality," and I defy you to look into its eyes. It is deadly. It rapes the spirit and destroys the mind.

The civil service mentality puts absolutely anything and everything ahead of work. This mentality thinks in the following way: "I don't need the public, the public needs me." Then: "I won't do one bit more than I have to do." And then: "Just because you ask for something doesn't mean you're going to get it, because I may have to use some energy." And finally: "It's not my job."

True, there are notable exceptions, but would to God that I was being facetious instead of merely verbose. And you, each of you, know what I'm saying is true because you've had to face the monster at the Social Security office, the IRS, the department of health, the driver's license bureau, and the post office. And let me add that this mentality isn't actually limited to the government. You can find it in major corporations and in public utility companies.

I've deliberately painted a dark picture here because I don't want you to be surprised, shocked, or discouraged by what you will find when you show up at the motor vehicles department or the post office or the county courthouse to do some research. The main message here is: It won't be easy. But, as I explained in Chapter Two, if you know what you want and what you're entitled to get, if you're persistent, you'll get it in the end. Here's a real-life example that proves the point.

A year or so ago I was working on a case in Florida that involved determining the whereabouts of the heirs to a substantial estate. During the course of the investigation I needed to verify the deaths of five members of the family, so I went to the appropriate office in the Dade County (Miami) Courthouse. I politely asked the clerk for what I needed, and she was extremely cooperative. In two minutes she was back holding five cards that contained the same information that was on the death certificates.

I took out my pen to copy down the dates on the cards and the clerk said, "You can't copy that information."

I groaned because it had been so easy up to that point. Then I thought to myself, "Of course, you jerk, don't you know that things can't be that easy?" But I said to her, "What do you mean I can't copy them? How am I supposed to get the information?"

"You can't copy them," she repeated.

"Will you make copies for me, then?" I asked in my most pleasant voice.

"No, I can't do that. It's against the rules," she said firmly.

"What am I supposed to do?" I said. She looked at me blankly and said nothing.

I needed the dates so I took another route.

"What if you read the information to me and I write it down?" I said. I thought that was pretty clever.

She didn't think so. "That's the same thing," she answered, and of course she was right.

But I stayed calm and then did something that I think was brilliant. I took one card, memorized what I needed, then went outside the office door and wrote the information down in my notebook. I did that five times. It was silly, and I must have looked absolutely ridiculous staring at a card and then hurrying outside and scribbling down some notes. But it got the job done, and it didn't break the rules.

Unfortunately, rules and regulations, however poorly conceived, govern the thought processes of the civil servant at every level of bureaucracy. In the case above they were perfectly willing to let you see the cards but not copy them. If I had known about this rule in advance I could have used a tape recorder and pretended I was reading the cards aloud to myself in order to memorize them while I was recording the information on my small pocket recorder. That would have looked and sounded pretty foolish too, but I would have had my information.

There are innumerable problems you're likely to face in your research, but there are two, both delaying tactics, that deserve special mention here. One is the mail delay and the other is the "working days" delay.

The first goes like this. You are told that you need to mail in a request for a form in order to receive the information you're seeking. The mail takes at least three days to get to its destination. The forms are probably not mailed for three days and then the return mail takes three days. You fill out the forms immediately, and you have another three-day mail delivery problem. It's now nearly two weeks, and you have still only requested the information. It may be anywhere from another week to a month before you get your answers.

The other delay is similar. When you ask the clerk for the information you get this answer: "That will take ten working days." Well, Rome was built in less time than that. If you are forced into one of these "ten working days" situations, I suggest that you call the office in question before you return to pick up your information, since the ten days often stretch to twelve or more. Our modern bureaucracy is a deadly combination of the worst elements of Kafka, Orwell, and *Catch-22*.

And this brings up another point you should know before beginning your research. Rules and regulations vary from state to state. What is public information in one city or one county or one state is private in another. In Florida, birth and death records are private, but by some strange twist in thinking, criminal records are available for all to see. In New York State almost all information is public except criminal records. Be aware that what can be gotten easily in one state may be impossible to get in another.

One more advisory. Where you begin your investigation depends on what you're looking for. Always sit down and analyze what it is that you want before you shoot off in the wrong direction and waste a lot of time.

Take this case. I was called by the owner of a steamship company and asked to meet with him.

When we sat down he said, "We have a million-dollar judgment against a Greek shipowner. He is ninety days overdue, and it's costing me money not to have that money. I want you to find his bank so we can file a lien and collect."

I said, "I'll save you a big fee. Just go to XYZ Bank."

"How do you know that?" he asked, "I haven't even told you the guy's name yet."

"Take my word for it," I said with conviction.

"Well, do the job anyway," he said, and as long as he was going to pay for it, I agreed to go ahead.

I made one phone call and sure enough, the account we wanted was at XYZ Bank. My client went to the bank, put a lien on the account, and collected his million bucks. Then he asked me, "How'd you do that so fast?"

"Easy," I said. "Virtually every Greek shipowner in the world has an account at that bank. It's more reliable than death and taxes."

The point is, I could have gone to the Maritime Court, which deals with issues involving ships in international waters or international disputes among shipowners. I could have spent a lot of time there and run up a bill and gotten the same information. But I knew I didn't need to take the long way. One thing, though. I don't want all you Greek shipowners going out and changing your accounts to other banks, OK?

Now let's take a closer look at some of the information that's available at each of the levels I mentioned above, always keeping in mind that access to records varies from state to state. In some places all of it is available and in others only some of it. It's a wildly variable situation. Also keep in mind that in different jurisdictions the same information may be available, but the method of retrieving it or the name of the office in which it is filed may be different. The federal system is consistent. If something is available in one place in the federal government, it is available from Maine to Hawaii and Alaska to Texas.

CITY

Every city or town of any size has telephone directories and libraries. If you're looking for someone, go to the phone book first and let your fingers do the walking. If the person lives in another city, the library will have out-of-town phone books, or you can call Information.

Probably the most valuable tool here is the *Cole's Directory*, which publishes householders' directories for every major metropolitan area in the United States and Canada. *Cole's* works in three ways:

1. If you have only a street address, you can look it up in the directory and you'll find the name and telephone number (if it is listed) of the person at that address.
2. If you have only the telephone number, you can find the number in the directory and it will give you the name and address of the person.
3. If you know the name, the directory works like a telephone book except that it also will show you the names and numbers of other people who live at that same address and give you an idea of the economic nature of that neighborhood. (*Cole's* uses symbols to indicate the relative affluence of an area.)

So *Cole's*, available in most libraries, will help you answer any of the following questions:

- Is there such an address?
- I know the address, but what is the phone number?
- I know the address, but what is the name?
- Who are the next-door neighbors?
- Who are the tenants of that apartment or office building?
- Is the address a business or a residential listing?

All of this information is valuable in the search for people and additional information.

For example, if you follow your husband or wife to an address and find that it's a large apartment building, you can use *Cole's* to check the names of the residents at that address. It is possible that one of those names will be familiar. Since *Cole's* also gives the phone numbers of the residents, you can call that familiar name and, using a ruse, confirm the residence of the person you want to identify.

Libraries also have a variety of journals produced by trade and professional associations, and these can yield valuable leads. For example, if you're looking for a specific doctor, the journal of the state medical association or the state office that regulates the medical profession will have a complete listing of doctors, including addresses and telephone numbers. The same is true of lawyers. A list of all practicing lawyers is kept by the state. One of the best sources is a book called the *Directory of Associations*, which lists virtually every association in the United States. It contains listings as diverse as toy buyers and Chinese-American singers, and for each listing it gives the number of members, the name of the president, the address, and the telephone number. I know about the Chinese-American Singers Association because I once had the job of finding a person of Chinese origin who was also a singer. This association, listed in the directory, helped me find that person. I have been a devoted fan of this directory ever since.

Also, don't neglect the local chamber of commerce, the tourism bureau, or any other agency in the city that is there to help the resident or the stranger.

Voter registration records may be kept in the city or the county, but whichever the place, they are usually public information. All you have to do is ask for it. The information available on a voter registration form can include name, date of birth, employer, and sometimes former addresses and where the person was naturalized. This is all valuable when you're trying to locate someone for whatever reason.

COUNTY

The county courthouse is perhaps the best single source of information on people. The county clerk's office, which may be divided into several departments, is the best single source in the courthouse. The secret is finding out which department within the clerk's office has what information, and this can take some experience.

The parking violations bureau has a listing of all parking tickets, and these tickets contain the make and year of the car, the license number, the time of day of the violation, and the address where the car was parked. In most areas this information is on computer. You can simply call the department of motor vehicles and they will tell you where to go and how to get the information. In some states there will be a nominal charge. This information can be particularly helpful in locating someone in New York, where parking violations are such a common occurrence. In fact, the famous "Son of Sam" murder case was finally solved through the parking violations bureau. An enterprising city detective decided to check to see if there had been a violation on any one car in the general area around which the murders took place. He found one vehicle with a violation at about the time of one of the murders. That car was later traced to the killer, David Berkowitz.

Also in the courthouse you'll find a list of judgments, which can provide clues about a person's background. Here, the name of the person is enough. If it is a common name, it is helpful to have an address, Social Security number, or date of birth for verification. Financial information can be found if you look at liens, and the surrogate's court can yield a variety of information on a person's financial health. This court also keeps the records of indigent deaths, so if you're looking for someone who has dropped completely out of sight, you may want to check their records.

The county offices also have the records of civil actions, marriages, deaths, births, estate probates, DBA (Doing Business As) filings (for example, a DBA on Irwin Blye might say doing business as Crazy Irwin), real estate transactions, deeds, mortgages, and pistol permits.

Certificates of incorporation can also be found in the county courthouse. If you want to know who the principal owner of Burke Clothing Co. is, the certificate of incorporation or business certificate will tell you who is involved in the business. There are sole-proprietorships, partnerships, and incorporations. There will be three separate listings, so you may have to check all three categories, but they will all be maintained in the same office.

STATE

I use the state department of motor vehicles in almost every case I work on because they issue driver's licenses. In New York a form must be filed and a small fee paid to get the information on the license, but it's worth it because the information I get includes the name, address, date of birth, height, weight, color of eyes, restrictions on the driver (for example, must wear corrective lenses when driving), make and year of car or cars owned, liens against the driver's car or cars, a list of moving violations, and a list of accidents including the names of the people involved, and possibly the place of employment of the car owner, and his or her Social Security number. With this wealth of information, it becomes relatively easy to trace a person.

Remember, these documents are matters of public record. You don't need to make up a story or give an excuse to anyone, because you're entitled to the information. The name of the form you need (and even the name of the division of government) may vary from state to state, but if you explain what it is you're looking for, the agency can tell you how to get it.

State supreme court records are available for review. Judgment records can prove very useful because they tell you the names of the plaintiffs and the defendants and all you will ever want or need to know about a given case. In most states the records of matrimonial cases are maintained in the supreme court. But in New York, for example, they are not considered public information, though you can obtain the court dockets, which list the parties involved in a matrimonial case and the attorneys for both parties.

The state liquor authority has a ton of financial and background information on people who apply for liquor licenses, since most states make an effort to keep organized crime and the criminal element in general out of the business of selling liquor. This is public information in many states.

I've found the Uniform Commercial Code or UCC to be a wonderful source of information. The UCC handles what used to be referred to as chattel mortgages, and a UCC filing records a lien against personal property. Such things as auto loans and home improvement loans are filed with the UCC by the finance companies and banks where the loans are obtained. The filing gives a name, address, a bank name, and data about other things you own like a boat, property, or jewelry. Remarkably, these filings are public, and anyone can look at them. They are particularly useful in background and financial investigations.

What's even more interesting to me is that I know there are things in the state court system that the public is entitled to know that I don't even know are there. Someday . . .

FEDERAL

Far from being secretive and closed, the federal government is an open source of information in many areas. The Social Security system will provide a massive amount of information to relatives and especially to parents, and all that's necessary is a Social Security number. Of course, you must prove you are a parent or relative, but after that you can obtain virtually all the information in a person's file.

The Immigration and Naturalization Service is also a good source if you're a relative of the person on whom you are seeking information. This is especially valuable for people tracing their genealogy. Forms are available in person or by mail from the local office of the INS.

Some naturalization records are available in the federal courts as well. These records tell when and where a person was born; who his parents were; when, where, and how he came to this country; his occupation; and his sponsors. It might even include the name of the boat on which the new immigrant arrived.

The last time I tried to get this information, however, I met face to face with one of those aforementioned civil servants with that aforementioned "mentality." I asked for the records on a client, and the following conversation took place.

Clerk: "Who are you and what do you want?"

I was immediately upset because I didn't expect any problem at all so I said, "My name is John Q. Public, and it's none of your business what I want or why I want it because it's a public record. And if you don't know that, then I suggest you ask your supervisor."

Clerk: "I'll ask."

Two minutes later she returned with the information. The point is, the information is public, you have a right to it, and there's no reason you shouldn't get it—though you may have to face difficulties or aggravation along the way.

By the way, the local public library can be a good source of genealogical information, and the Church of Jesus Christ of the Latter-day Saints in Salt Lake City, Utah, maintains an entire mountain cave filled with data on virtually every immigrant to this country since the late 1800s. A telephone call to their central office will get you the right referral.

Federal records—civil, criminal, bankruptcy, maritime proceedings, stock listings, and stock certificates—are maintained at a United States district courthouse. If there was a federal action in any of these areas, the information will be in that building. Federal criminal actions like Securities and Exchange Commission fraud, mail fraud, and other post office violations are also in the district court. Federal tax liens, which give names, addresses, and other information, are also public and can be found in federal court buildings in most cities. All you have to do is ask for federal tax lien information and it will be yours. This information is valuable in background checks and financial investigations for business or matrimonial reasons.

The Securities and Exchange Commission is a great source of information on public companies, stockbrokers, and investment advisers. Every public company must file a mass of forms with the SEC. So if you want to know the financial condition of any public company, who the officers are, and something about the background of the principals you will find it at the SEC. Furthermore, if the company is involved in any litigation, that has to be reported to the SEC, and it is also public. To take advantage of this agency's resources you'll need to go directly to the SEC and search the records, or write for the data you need by using a form that the SEC will provide on request.

Three other sources at the SEC are:

• The SEC Litigation Index, which lists anyone involved in litigation directly with the SEC. A lot of legitimate brokers as well as wheeler-dealers, con men, and fraud artists have had problems with the SEC, and this is where you'll find their names and their modes of operation.

• The Broker-Dealer File, which lists everyone registered as a broker-dealer with the SEC. These people must submit financial statements as well as a personal biography on every principal in the company. This biography includes at least ten years of background information, the degree of ownership of company, birth date, Social Security number, education, and much more.

• The Investment Adviser File, which has some of the same information as above on those people who are registered as investment advisers.

The post office maintains the forwarding address of everyone who files one in what is called the "removal book." This book is kept for two years and after that any letter to the former address is marked "not forwardable." A forwarding address is public information, and the clerk at the post office is obliged to give it to you. It's also good to know that the removal books more than two years old are probably kept in the basement of the post office rather than destroyed, though you'll get the refrain that the old books have been burned. If the clerk gives you a hard time you can always say, "I'm requesting this under the Freedom of Information Act." This has worked for me in the past, but it depends on your attitude, because the clerk does not have to comply with your request after the forwarding period has expired. In that case you may have to write a letter to the Post Office Department, but you *can* eventually get that address.

GENERAL

For almost every industry and every professional field there are places to go for information. If you're interested in buying into a business you can determine the legitimacy of that business and its solvency by researching the various credit organizations that serve that industry. For example, the clothing industry has its own credit organization, and so do most other industries. The general credit services, such as Dun & Bradstreet, can also provide useful information. One of Dun & Bradstreet's divisions, for example, the National Credit Organization (which most people have not heard of), specializes in mobile home dealers. You will have to pay for this information, and the person or business you are inquiring about will be notified that there has been an inquiry. The Jewelers Board of Trade is the place to go for information on the jewelry industry.

The 1980s have brought us a new and wonderful information tool and plunked it down right on our desks. It's within reach of everyone, and it's called the personal computer. With a PC and a communications modem you can sit in your home or office and gain immediate access to an incredible variety of information. From psychological studies on suicide in Yugoslavia to the latest scores from the world of sports, you can tap out your needs and get your answers without working up a sweat or wearing out a pair of shoes. In fact, you don't even have to wear shoes as you explore the entire world's store of knowledge and data. It is all literally at your fingertips.

All of this information is available through the various computer data base services to which you can subscribe for a modest fee. There are services that are general and services that specialize in such fields as the law or medicine. As a nonprofessional investigator, you probably won't make use of the specialty services, but some of the other data bases can save time and energy. You can find books in print, abstracts of magazine and newspaper articles, reports on the effects of exposure to chemical substances, lists of corporate boards of directors, a compendium of federal research projects, who is who in this country and abroad, and much more. This information can be valuable in all types of investigations, and you will be limited only by your investigation and the amount of money you can afford to add to your telephone bill, since the real cost of obtaining the information you need comes in the fees charged by the services for accessing from a particular data bank and for the telephone transmission of that information. It's easy to run up a big bill if you just sit down to play. On the other hand, you can save hours, even weeks, of time by tickling the keyboard.

Another source of data base information—but one that does the research for you and supplies that information to you—is called Disclosure. Their offices are located in Washington, D.C., and they will get you almost any report you can dream of for a fee of twenty or thirty dollars. If you need the information immediately, they will send it by express mail and you can have it overnight. This, of course, saves you the cost of buying a computer, but it also takes away some of the fun, since you don't get to play around with all that data yourself.

A valuable sourcebook was written by a former CIA agent a number of years ago. Called *Where's What*, it focuses on what is where in the government, but it also contains data about public agencies as well. It is out of print now, but it is still available in libraries.

A FEW FINAL WORDS OF WISDOM ABOUT RESEARCH

1. In many cases it is easier to get information if you're a woman. That may sound sexist, but it's the truth. I've seen it too many times. There I am trying to get a little help, a tiny piece of information, and getting absolutely nowhere, when a female colleague walks up, smiles, holds out her hand, and gets the whole ball of wax.

2. In all the background investigations I've done, and there have been hundreds, there was only one person on whom I couldn't find anything. I could turn up absolutely nothing in all the sources mentioned above or in others I also tried. Not one iota of information could I find. I felt as if I was banging my head against a wall, and then I realized that all of this was telling me something. It told me the man didn't exist, that apparently I had been given a phony name, and the man I was looking for wasn't real. That taught me that if I'm really up against a dead end, I should start considering the fact that I'm on a phony trail. So remember that even a lack of information tells you something. In other words, a lack of information can give you a positive answer.

3. In the end you can probably find out something about anybody, especially if you're willing to pay for it. But with no money at all, you can find out a great deal if you are patient and determined.

And finally, remember what I said about privacy? Remember that I said there was no such thing? Well, now do you believe me?

12

Equipment:
Low Tech and No Tech

Uzi submachine guns, "Dirty Harry" pistols, infrared sniper scopes, ultrasensitive listening devices, minibugs, micro–tape recorders, 35mm cameras with superlong lenses, videotape cameras and recorders with long-range microphones are the stuff of James Bond. I wish I could tell you that PIs use this kind of hardware, but we don't.

I enjoy watching movies with high-tech gadgets because I love high-tech gadgets. I have a microwave oven, an exercise bike with a pulse monitor, a remote control TV and VCR, a calculator that talks, a personal computer, a fancy camera, and a lot of other electronic toys I hardly ever touch, including one of the first versions of Pac-Man. But the fact is, the fancy gimmicks work much better for the CIA, the KGB, Interpol, Scotland Yard, and other agencies involved in international intrigue than they do for the PI trying to do an ordinary matrimonial in the Borough of Queens, New York. I must admit that while I'm watching a snoop on TV put a bug in someone's martini glass, I fantasize about doing the same thing. The only problem is, it takes very sophisticated and expensive equipment to pick up the message from that submerged bug, and I'm pretty certain the message is usually about as informative as: "I don't know, Marty, what do you want to do tonight?"

Maybe someday I'll be able to afford and, more important, find a use for these goodies, but in the meantime I have to work with what I've got and what I need. Some of the equipment that I use I've already told you about, but I'll review it all here. The reality is that for me there are only two kinds of equipment necessary to conduct my business—the basic and the basic plus one.

How basic is basic? Well, can you get more basic than a pencil and paper? I always carry a small notebook and pencils and pens because I never know when I'm going to have to quickly scribble down a license number, an address or telephone number, a description of a car or human, or the name of that Italian restaurant I just passed that looked so good. For me, the best thing about a notebook and pen is that the batteries never run out and the tape is never used up. You can always find a scrap of paper somewhere, but you can't always dig up a spare set of AA batteries when you need them.

Another basic piece of equipment is a pair of sunglasses. Shades are indispensable, and they serve three vital functions. The first is the one they were designed for, that is, to keep the sun out of your eyes. The second use for sunglasses is to obscure the movement of your eyes. People are disconcerted by dark sunglasses; mirrored glasses are even more confusing, but they seem too affected to me. Behind dark glasses people can't tell if you're looking at them or at the striking brunette standing right behind them. This allows your eyes to roam at will. And since people can't make eye contact, they can't easily identify you when you show up later in an elevator without your glasses. Finally, sunglasses serve as a minimal disguise. Put on a pair of sunglasses, and you'll see how much they change the way you look. Unless they're some weird shape or color they don't attract much attention, and in fact they seem to cause people's eyes to bounce off you. Be judicious, however. Don't wear dark shades in a dimly lighted nightclub or at a brightly lighted cocktail party. Remember, you should not be conspicuous. So, I always use sunglasses in the sun, and I use them with care and discretion, as the situation demands.

And now, here's some good news for the hat industry. Next to sunglasses, a hat is the best disguise because it changes your appearance radically. Humphrey Bogart was rarely seen without a hat rakishly pulled down over one eye. Though I don't follow that style, I too wear a hat much of the time. Almost any kind will do as long as it isn't too strange looking. If you have a striking hair color or hairstyle, or if you're bald or very gray, a hat makes all the difference. On the other hand, if you normally wear a hat, you should change the style or take it off. The idea is to appear a bit different from the way you normally appear. I'd say "use your head," but that might be too corny.

The next item on my list of necessities is a tape recorder, tapes, and batteries. While the notebook is good, a recorder is like, "Look ma, no hands." You can make notes without taking your hands off the steering wheel and your eyes off the road and the car you're following. This also applies to foot surveillance. If you stop to make a note, or look away for a few seconds, your subject can disappear, never to be seen again. So, despite their shortcomings—they can be bulky and conspicuous—recorders are valuable and basic tools. I recommend a small, inexpensive model that fits in your pocket and has simple control buttons that you can use without looking at them. Use 120 minute tapes so you won't have to reach casually into your pocket to try to change a tape in the middle of a conversation.

A slightly more advanced piece of equipment can also be useful, and even though it is high tech, it isn't very expensive. I'm talking about what we call a body recorder. Let's face it, there is nothing unobtrusive about reaching into your briefcase and turning on a tape recorder. The solution to this problem is a small, voice-activated tape recorder that can be taped to the body or carried in an inside coat pocket. Voice activation theoretically means that the machine will start recording when it is activated by a human voice. But, of necessity, the machine must be sensitive, so in practice it starts or reacts to any kind of noise with sufficient volume. If you use this kind of machine your tape will be full of extraneous noise, but you still should have what you need. It also has the advantage of being small and unobtrusive.

Next, I'd invest in a powerful but inexpensive pair of binoculars. They should be small enough not to be easily spotted by someone, and if they can fit into your coat pocket so much the better. Get as much power as you can because it will allow you to stay farther away from your subject, which makes you harder to spot—a major advantage when you're on a surveillance.

Earlier I mentioned keeping a camera in the glove compartment because a picture is worth a thousand words. If you want to use a good camera for your investigative work that's fine, but a simple auto-focus model will do the job perfectly and you won't miss something while you twist the dials and set shutter speeds.

Recently I've added a slightly more sophisticated piece of electronic equipment to my kit. I've taken to using an electronic phone beeper—not for the purpose of notifying me of telephone calls, but as a signaling device. It's useful in the following kind of situation. Say I'm maintaining a surveillance down the block from where my subject is likely to be. He may be leaving his apartment or house, getting into an elevator, or going to the garage to pick up his car. Someone in a position to see what is going on observes this and then calls me on my beeper. I know by the signal that my subject will be coming into sight soon, and I'm ready to move when he does. This may be a little sophisticated for the amateur, but it is very effective.

But back to the basics.

We're going to talk next about a slightly delicate subject—going to the bathroom. When you're on a surveillance the body continues to function in its normal manner, if you get my meaning. That means that unless you want to be in pain or cause a terrible mess, you will have to go to the bathroom on a fairly regular basis. What to do? You can't leave your position because that is exactly the time your subject is going to appear. It never fails, believe me. The alternative is the wide-mouthed, plastic bottle that I described earlier, the most important piece of equipment of all. It isn't particularly attractive or comfortable to use this kind of urinal, but it isn't comfortable to sit in a car for hours on end and not be able to go to the bathroom either. Women will have more of a problem than men, but they too can use the bottle. I know it can be done.

Buy two flashlights. One of them should be small so that it can be kept in your pocket and used inconspicuously. You'll also need a more powerful model that will give you sufficient light to walk with if you find yourself in a dark basement or hallway. Both sizes will come in handy because it can get very dark out there.

A small pocket knife is also a good thing to carry. You never know when you may have use for a little blade, and it will be useful for trimming your hangnails on those long, uneventful surveillances.

As long as we're at it, let's talk a bit about some of the more affordable yet exotic pieces of equipment you might want to buy. Since video cameras have become so portable and relatively affordable, I've invested in a complete outfit, including the connection that plugs into the lighter in my car. I use it primarily on surveillances, but occasionally it comes in handy in the office for in-house training sessions. It's lightweight, works in low light, and has rechargeable batteries. I admit it isn't essential, but it's a nice piece of hardware that actually can be useful.

Finally, there's the personal computer. I never believed in the things until a client of mine gave me one in lieu of a fee. We now use it to keep records, but for me, the most useful function is the ability to access (that's computer talk) data-base information on everything from library books to government documents.

13

How to Hire a Private Eye

I'd like to say that I don't think this chapter is necessary. I'd like to think that in all these pages I've given you enough solid information to do your own investigations.

But I know that isn't true, because even after thirty years, there are times when I have to hire a specialist for a particular job in my own field. And remember, I said at the outset that I was not going to be able to teach you everything there is to know about being a private eye.

True, I've given you enough of the basic tools to allow you to do many things—including matrimonial investigations, locates, simple surveillances, and research. But there are some investigative jobs that even the professional finds difficult—which means that they can be murder for the amateur.

In other words, I still believe there comes a time in everyone's life when they need the services of a professional private investigator. When that time comes for you, I want you to be able to make an intelligent choice. I want you to be able to find a person who will get the job done efficiently and at the right price.

When I hire a new investigator to work for me I look for certain professional and personal qualities, and I advise you to do the same. For me those qualities, not necessarily in the order of their importance, are training, experience, competence, reputation, honesty, expertise, and professionalism. These are the qualities to look for when you go out to hire a private investigator. None of these traits is assurance of a good job, but they are better than leafing through the yellow pages and finding the biggest advertisement. Which is, by the way, the absolutely worst way to find the person you want.

Let's examine these qualities one at a time.

Training. Like doctors, lawyers, dentists, and other professionals, private investigators have all received some professional training somewhere. PIs naturally come from a variety of backgrounds, but most are educated (many are college graduates) and most have had some training in law enforcement. Former police officers and government agents gravitate to this sort of work, either after retirement or sooner, if they have become tired of routine work or they see the opportunity to make more money in private investigation. Those PIs who haven't been in some law enforcement agency have, more often than not, learned on the job, and there is not a thing wrong with that. I got most of my training on the job.

When you go to see a PI, don't look for any diplomas on the wall that indicate a degree from PI University because no place exists. There have been, and are, schools that teach the rudiments of the profession, but none offers a formal degree program. But all legitimate private investigators have to obtain a license issued by the state where they work. We all had to pass a test to get that license, and the legitimate PI will show you his license at your request.

Licensing doesn't imply training, however, so don't be confused. Anyone who can pass the test can get a license, whether they've had a day of training or not. I know half a dozen people who have taken the licensing exam just for fun and passed it. Let's face it, it isn't all that difficult. But they've never gone any further in their training. They just like to carry the piece of paper around in their wallets to show off from time to time.

Experience. Experience and training are not the same thing. You can train a soldier to perfection, but there is nothing like the experience of battle. Battle-tested soldiers are the ones you want to stay close to. Since there is not much available in the way of formal training for the private eye, experience is gained in the field. The tricks of the trade, so to speak, are the result of actual case experience.

Therefore, I suggest that the PI you hire have a minimum of three years' experience and be able to document it. If this PI runs his or her own investigation business, the business should be at least two years old.

Don't hesitate to ask for references, and be sure to get half a dozen names so that they aren't all personal friends.

Competence. You'll get an idea of an investigator's competence when you talk to his references, but I think that, to a degree, you can also judge competence by the way the investigator's office looks, the way he speaks, the questions he asks, the way he takes notes, and the amount of self-confidence he shows. You don't want a wimp or a head-basher. You want someone who is confident in his skills and has a track record to prove it. The ultimate test of competence, of course, is the way the investigator handles your case, but you won't know that until after you get started. Use your instincts here. If you have a good feeling, then you're probably making the right choice.

Reputation. You should not only check an investigator's references, but check with the private investigator's organization in your area. It's something like a trade association and will not only make recommendations but may even advise you about the members. You might try to make some inquiries of other professionals—lawyers, and even other PIs—who have used the man or woman you finally select. You might even call a competitor and say that you are thinking of hiring a certain private investigator and ask what he or she thinks about your choice. If a competitor has praise for your man (or at least nothing terribly critical to say), then you know you've made a good selection.

Honesty. Diogenes, the Greek philosopher, spent a good part of his life looking far and wide for an honest man, and I don't remember if he ever found one. Judging honesty before the fact is even more difficult than evaluating most of the other intangibles we've just enumerated. When it comes to this trait, you'll have to rely again on your instincts. Does the investigator give you a firm handshake and look you in the eye? Does he try to sell you a service you don't need? Do you get a good feeling? Even if you are satisfied with his behavior on all these points, be careful. I've met guys who give you a good feeling, who have firm handshakes, who look you right in the eye and only sell you what you need, and they have been thieves. Honesty is as honesty does, I suppose.

Expertise. If you have a heart condition you go to a cardiologist. If you have a tax problem you go to an accountant. If you can't get your backhand over the net you go to the club tennis pro. It's the same in investigation. I often hire a specialist because I know that I'm better at some things than at others. A specialist, a guy with expertise, can save you a tremendous amount of time and money because he knows how to do the job.

There's the old story about the company that calls in a computer expert to fix their million-dollar computer. He takes one quick look at the computer and taps it twice on the side with a small hammer. The machine lights up and runs beautifully. He then sends in a bill for $5,000. The company is outraged because he was only there for five minutes. They ask for a breakdown of the charges. The specialist writes back: "Time—$100; knowing where to hit the machine—$4,900."

The same is true in my business. If a PI knows where to hit the machine he may charge you a little more, but he saves you a lot of money in the long run. So, determine what you need, and if you need a specialist, don't go to a generalist. Most PIs will admit it if they don't feel capable of handling a case.

Professionalism. By professionalism I don't mean wearing a gun and a trench coat and sucking a lollipop. It isn't a matter of appearances. Professionalism involves all the other traits I've mentioned above, but it also involves the manner and the dispatch with which a case is handled. It means regular phone calls to you and the prompt return of your phone calls. It means itemized expense statements and itemized hourly charges. It means prompt

186 ■ *Secrets of a Private Eye*

and carefully written reports. It means keeping all aspects of your case in absolute confidence. It means an efficient office.

All this is a little hard to judge before a job. After the job is over it's too late, but you'll know if your case was handled professionally.

How do you find someone with all those sterling qualities? This is one time you don't let your fingers do the walking through the phone book. The best way to find a PI is through a referral from someone you know and trust. If you mention to several friends that you are looking for a private investigator, one of them is going to have had personal experience with a private investigator or know someone who has.

After you get a referral, call the PI and arrange an appointment, preferably in his office. You want to steer clear of the fly-by-night operator, the guy who works out of his bedroom, or the person who dabbles on the weekends. This is serious business, and it should be conducted as business, not as a sideline.

In the end, the only way to tell if you have the right person is to conduct your own interview. Lay out the particulars of your case and then judge the response. In reality, you're interviewing someone for a job.

There is one final consideration in choosing a private investigator—the fee. Contrary to popular opinion, most cases don't take that long. I can often finish a difficult case in a few hours. This always amazes the client, and sometimes he or she feels cheated because I was able to do it so easily. But that is expertise. I'd say that the majority of my cases take an average of three days. Beware of the guy who says, "This looks like a very difficult case. I'm afraid it will take several weeks." Unless it's a very strange situation, the guy is a phony and trying to milk you.

Most PIs charge by the hour and, though fees vary from city to city and state to state, they fall within a fairly narrow range for standard investigations. There is a much wider price range of fees when it comes to special situations.

Good hunting.

PI Lexicon

aka	also known as
bad paper	stolen or counterfeit securities or money
bomber	powerful matrimonial attorney
bread	money, loot
brick	marijuana or hashish in brick form
bulldog	opposite of pavement artist
burn	to be identified as a tail
bust	to arrest
chesty	feeling strong in your own head; full of authority
chicken	homosexual term for a young boy
chickenhawk	adult male homosexual with preference for young boys; also hawk
collar	arrest
connection	source of drugs
cowboy	unlicensed private eye
deck	small bag of heroin
docket numbers	criminals or criminal types
DMV	department of motor vehicles
DWI	driving while impaired
fence	criminal receiver of stolen property
flimflam	all types of confidence games

glass (also ice)	jewelry
head	marijuana user
holding	possessing a controlled substance
hot paper	stolen money or securities
Johnson	stolen vehicle
joint	marijuana cigarette; prison
junkie	narcotics addict
key	a kilo (2.2 pounds) of drugs
lid	small bag of marijuana
LKA	last known address
make	to identify
off	to get rid of something or someone
on the job	term used to identify a private eye or a policeman at work
pavement artist	a smooth operator
pirate tap	illegal phone tap
short eyes	child molester
strung out	addicted
tag	parking summons
tail	to follow, conduct surveillance
tipped	altered credit card
toss	to frisk or search
wise guy	member of a Mafia family
works	narcotics implements
zinger	a summons

Investigator Associations

Associated Licensed Detectives of New York State
1806 East Avenue
Rochester, NY 14610

Associated Special Investigators and Police International
P.O. Box 434
Saint John, New Brunswick, Canada

Council of International Investigators
311 Oak Grove Drive
P.O. Box 2712
Akron, OH 44319

International Association of Arson Investigators
25 Newton Street
P.O. Box 600
Marlboro, MA 01752

International Association of Chiefs of Police
13 Firstfield Road
Gaithersburg, MD 20878

National Council of Investigation and Security
P.O. Box 433
Severna, MD 21146

Society of Professional Investigators
1120 E. 31st Street
Brooklyn, NY 11210

World Association of Detectives
P.O. Box 36174
Cincinnati, OH 45236

Index